T0131699

# Sex Trends in Society

Kathy S. Thompson, M.A.,
Education and Counseling

authorHOUSE

*AuthorHouse™*
*1663 Liberty Drive*
*Bloomington, IN 47403*
*www.authorhouse.com*
*Phone: 833-262-8899*

*The author makes no claim to the accuracy of details in this book. The author has attempted to remove any*
*noted errors and has checked out what could be checked out as well as possible. Efforts towards accuracy have*
*been made but the author makes no claim to there being full and complete accuracy of the book's contents.*

*Published by AuthorHouse 02/24/2022*

*ISBN: 978-1-7283-5863-5 (sc)*
*ISBN: 978-1-7283-5862-8 (e)*

*Library of Congress Control Number: 2020906339*

*Print information available on the last page.*

*This book is printed on acid-free paper.*

# Edubooks by Kathy S. Thompson

## Poems and Short Works Books (57 in each)

Going through Life Poems and Short Works
Getting through Life Poems and Short Works
Next Poems and Short Works
Straggler Poems and Short Works
Isolates Poems and Short Works
Extra Poems and Short Works
Final Poems and Short Works
Spare Poems and Short Works
Subsequent Poems and Short Works

## Young Readers Books

Charlie and Mom Cat (early readers)
The Cygnet (young readers and all ages)
Madame Spider (tweens, teens, and all ages))
Philpot and the Forest Animals (young readers, and all ages)

# Disclaimer

The author makes no claim to the accuracy of details in this book. The author has attempted to remove any noted errors and has checked out what could be checked out as well as possible. Efforts towards accuracy have been made but the author makes no claim to there being full and complete accuracy of the book's contents. Any errors brought to the attention of the author will be corrected in the future.

# Contents

# *Apology*

I know this book is not perfectly written. Though I majored in English as an undergraduate, I've forgotten some grammar, plus some grammar and even spelling rules have changed over the years and I have not kept up with those new ways, although, many of them are optional. Still, grammar can get to be a little muddled in the mind. So, apologies for any and all imperfections. Just getting the book out was the priority. Therefore, you may find some irregularity, in that the book was not professionally edited. I hope there's no typing errors (but my eyes are not so good). So, apologies go out for any and all oversights or undersights. There may be some repetition, too. Some is purposely there, to drive in a point. Some is accidentally there but is put in a different context. Because I was working on more than one book at a time, I would sometimes forget what I had already written so I occasionally put the same information in twice—almost always in a different context. Also, this book was a bit of a rush job. Because the book was somewhat rushed, all sentence construction may not be immaculate but most of the content generally makes sense in so far as I know.

Furthermore, you may think some text information does not directly relate to the included covered subjects. There is, perhaps, some borderline material in there. With what may seem extraneous, if you give it more thought, you would likely make the connection that the material does relate to the overall subject and certainly to what is generally being covered in the text. There are one or two covered areas that may be more remotely related to the principal subject but I wanted to add in those subjects and felt that they were connected. All points made tie in with the overall subject, and they generally or specifically relate. Some points that were made do, more than others. I tried to be thorough; I am a detail-oriented writer. Putting so many details in so the book would be more comprehensive was not always so easy to do and so the organization of the book is not quite all that I would have wanted it to be, but I'm not unhappy with it. Mainly, I got everything in that I wanted in and that was my priority. Again, this book was a little rushed.

Also, a computer tech caused me to lose material, relative to my final draft, after it had been done. Consequently, there are some omissions and could be some errors. I had very little time to re-correct. I lost some good additions, too.

# Chapter 1

# Comparative Sexualities and Marriage

Ideas, beliefs, values, attitudes, and feelings shift, pendulums swing, and lifestyles change. With reference to male and female sexuality, we, as a society, don't think the same things that we used to think thirty or so years ago (and even less years than that). Roles are different, new laws have been passed, culture has changed, and some of our traditions have been fading. Even new medical surgeries are being performed. Some have been performed for a while and some haven't, because they are so new. Men can become women, physically and anatomically, and women can become men, physically and anatomically.

In the American society (versus certain others), people are free to think what they want and do what they want so detachment about other people's choices is best. There are latent pressures and desires that each person has, at given times. Each person has the right to be them, and to change or not change . . . in whatever the direction. Is there too much freedom? That would depend on what the standards are, but standards must stand on their merit. Standards reflect the times. Should standards change, or stay as they are? Are their higher standards, and lower standards? Who is to be final judge of standards? This is what is at-issue, and it probably always will be.

Some people do not think about standards, and do not even live by a moral code, but everybody should establish their own foundation of life, when they can. More consistent decisions will be made, after they do. People like to experiment and try what is new and even off-beat (especially, the younger people do). People want to learn about life. They want to find happiness. Frankly, some of the young people do not, yet, know how hard it is to live in this world. They often get forced into situations, as they are trying to find themselves and learn about the world. They can get trapped, and stuck. Some will go to jail. Some will end out in court. Some will get hooked on drugs, and some will over-dose. Some will get into wrong relationships.

They may marry, then divorce. Early years can be chaos, and a learning journey. Some young people know very little, when they start out.

In this day and age, young people do not have it so good. They need more help than the previous generation did. They are experiencing much frustration . . . and it doesn't matter the race, color, or creed. The times are harder. They are confusing. There are fewer perks and breaks now, than there once were. Many turn to sex, when looking for stability and happiness. More gay people are out in the open and in some states, they can be legally married.

Only some transvestites decide to be gay. Quite a few are bisexual, or they say they are (but may not really be). A transvestite is a person who wishes to dress like, and act like someone of the opposite sex. There is more tolerance towards transvestites now. It has become a 'live and let live' world--at least it has, up to a point. There are controls, here and there, but everyone has to live within controls and laws. If they don't, they're wrong and impatient. There are also freedoms.

The number of transvestites has increased in society. Gay rights have flooded many cultures. There are transvestites who are crossdressers, and some transvestites decide to have a sex-change operation because they are not satisfied with their gender. After a sex-change operation, these people essentially become lesbians or homosexuals, in an indirect way, since they'd been born a different sex than what they now are. But since they have medically gone through a sex change, and are now the sex they want to be, they are not exactly lesbians or homosexuals (per se), so the coin has two sides about this issue. Their sex change conforms to their sexual identity.

A sex change is referred to as gender re-assignment. It is expensive, and usually a series of different operations are needed for full gender re-assignment but not all go that route and will end out having only some gender re-assignment operations. Sex identity does not always relate to sexual preference.

Sexual preference is something that goes in different directions these days, more so than in years gone by. There is more permissiveness and acceptance about these things, or at least, more tolerance. In some cases, tolerance is on the surface. Religious people cannot be forced to compromise their beliefs. Beliefs are more meaningful to some, less meaningful to others. They are relative, but also, even within the same religion, different people see things differently. Gender identity is an issue. Some people who were born as one sex identify with another sex. Some males really do have some feminine characteristics; many females really do have some masculine characteristics. There are some who want to change their gender even when they do not have conflicting gender characteristics. People have the legal right to choose their own gender identity, regardless of their at-birth gender. People have the legal right to choose how they want to sexually partner with someone and today, there are more gays in the world than ever before, mainly in the free and democratic world. There are also more open gays.

The gay life is not accepted in Muslim countries. Predominantly Catholic countries teach against being gay and there are considerably fewer gays, per capita, in such countries. In America, there are strict Catholics and there are non-strict Catholics, when it comes to keeping to actual scripture. Some scripture can be looked at in different ways; other scripture cannot. Scripture can have different applications. Many will go with other teachings, from other religions, when it comes to views about gender.

Relative to gay couples, on occasion one of the partners is a partial or a total transgender, which means, in all likelihood, that they've had at least some transgender-related surgery. A transvestite can also be gay, but may not necessarily be. More often, a transvestite is not a trans-sexual. Some men try women's clothes on, in jest, and out of interest, but they are not transvestites, in the more true sense of the word. It may have been a non-serious activity for them, but a few men are drawn to wearing women's clothes, in large part because they identify with the feminine gender. They want to keep on wearing women's clothes. You could, perhaps, even say it is a compulsion for them to wear women's clothes. It isn't just 'fun', 'experimental', or 'a lark'. This is also the case with women who put on men's clothing. Some may dabble with this reversal of clothing or cross-dressing but lose interest in it and drop it. For some, though, it becomes an obsession, for their own personal reasons, some of which can be deeply-rooted.

A transvestite is usually a male who adopts the dress, make-up, and hair of the opposite sex. They may also take on feminine behaviors. It can go the other way, too—i.e. women take on the dress, etc., and the behaviors of men. A transvestite isn't necessarily transgender because a trans-sexual goes beyond just the dressing and clothes wearing because they have a psychological urge to actually be the opposite sex and they may, then, have transgender surgery of various types. Many cosmetic procedures are sought after, to match the appearance of the opposite gender, and a transgender may go so far as to have their sex organs modified. Again, many transvestites are not trans-sexual and never go in that direction. Also, a number of transvestites will not allow themselves to be seen in public looking like a member of the opposite sex. Other transvestites don't mind ever being seen looking like a member of the opposite sex.

This is not set in stone, though. A transvestite male may even go out in public, dressed as a woman. So often, at gay rallies and parades, the men you see in female garb are not really trans-sexual. Some of them aren't even transvestites but will dress like that (in rallies and parades) just so they can make a pro-gay statement. Collectively, they all pack an image punch. You see a few women dressed as men at these rallies/parades, too—but not as many. Sometimes celebrities who are gay go to these rallies and parades. Some of these have been top celebrities, and are very beloved. Again, a transvestite can be a female who wears men's clothes and adopts men's looks, which can include haircut and style but some women who don't really think all that much about gender will wear more masculine-looking clothing, simply because they like the look and/or practicality of the clothes. You cannot assume that women who wear such clothing are transvestites. More women are getting more top jobs these days and so more suits and pant-suits are being worn.

With a trans-sexual, the individual becomes like the opposite sex (to what they are), particularly in the arenas of behaviors, actions, and activities. They have not had anything done, medically, to change their sex, but in other ways and mentally, they have changed over to the opposite sex. They can also be dual-sexual or bisexual and shift from the one sex to the other whenever they want to or whenever they must. An individual who is trans-genders has taken one or more steps to physically and medically change their sex and they are obviously already psychologically acclimated to perceiving themselves as being the opposite sex to their birth sex.

Today, there are more open same-sex relationships. They've been on the increase and became more noticeable around the turn of the 21st Century. Because of the increase in the number of gay people, in general, more gays wanted to be married (to each other) but they had been thwarted in their attempts, more often than not. Little by little, more states began to accept that gay couples had a constitutional right to be married and to have all related legal privileges and entitlements that are associated with marriage, which would include the areas of taxes, insurance, inheritance, right of survivorship, et al. Finally, so many states had agreed to same-sex marriage that the Supreme Court agreed to it in 2015. That's the historical chronology of gay marriage in a nutshell. So now, whenever 'married couple' is ever used, it can include the same-sex couples. Husband and wife are less frequently used words than spouse or married partner when it comes to same-sex married couples. Partner is the word used most often for same-sex relationships outside of marriage. (It is also used when referring to a couple of the opposite sex.) There are not many legally-married gay couples compared with what is termed straight couples, but since the Supreme Court decision, more gay couples have been getting married.

A monogamous marriage—two people, male and female—has been the primary sexual preference for the greatest majority of people. Males prefer females and females prefer males. Basically, monogamy is still the number one preference, but some people see coupling with someone as not being possible or as being undesirable, at least for themselves. One reason is because of 'career'. Some prefer being single or must be single, but not by choice. The trend around the turn of the Century was for people to couple up and to be married and live together and have children—sometimes a number of them. Many unmarried people live together today, and they even have children. This, too, is a new trend and the different religions look at this differently. Christianity sees it as a no, don't do. So does Judaism, and the Muslim and Hindu Faiths, in accordance with their literal laws.

Individuals who are paired up refer to themselves as a couple, partners, significant others, soul-mates, and/or marrieds. On occasion the word, friends, is used. Whether the relationship is heterosexual or homosexual, these are the words used to refer to paired-up people in a committed relationship. The word, partner, has been increasingly used by everyone—those who are in the relationship and those who are outside of the relationship (i.e. the word is used by friends and relatives). The word, partner, has significant connotation. It implies and connotes equality. It is used by those in a committed relationship, whether they are a married or unmarried couple.

Some people who are living together have no intention of ever getting married, but some do, and they follow through with it. Many women choose to live by themselves and to put career before marriage. It is an actual choice. Other women simply cannot find a man who they can love and get married to. Women not only have to learn how to take care of themselves these days, but they sometimes have to take care of their children, by themselves. For many, government aid is available. There can be full government aid, and partial government aid. Some are able to secure child support, and less often, alimony, assuming they were previously married. Quite often today, when women are coupled, they are making more money than their partner is making. In each relationship, this tide can always turn and sometimes does.

In any relationship, there can be sexism. Sexism occurs when one person in the relationship who is, or who perceives themselves as being a particular sex puts themselves into the superior position because they believe their gender is superior to the other sex. Consequently, they treat the other person as if they were inferior. Sexism has gone on since the beginning of relationships. Because men were bigger and stronger, they got away with sexism. We are more advanced now and men cannot, so readily, get away with mistreating, dominating, controlling, and abusing women. Laws are now in place, as is public opinion because of public values. Women have equal place. Sexism is an outdated view and practice, though it will, at times, be seen here and there. Roles in relationships can still be present, without sexism. This is the point. Many of society's views are now outdated and are faded or fading out.

True, some society views are still around and some of the 'older' ways are good and are worth holding on to. Most people want the good ones to stay and the bad ones to go . . . and the bad ones are going, but not, necessarily, all around the world. If it is defined and studied, people have a better chance of avoiding it, in a relationship. It is not handsome or pretty. It can be quite ugly. It can destroy a relationship. It can cause great unhappiness.

Sexism can go male to female, which is the more common type, or it can go female to male. It can be in any kind of relationship. When sexism is present, there's no sharing or not enough sharing. There's no respect or very little respect. This is because one person in a relationship sees themselves as superior to the other sex because of their own sex and so they want to be, and usually are dominant. They tend to want to control everything, which would include the other person in the relationship.

Western cultures tend to see relationships as being 50-50. Women gained equal rights over the years and they have no desire to go in reverse, legally or socially. They fought hard to acquire equal rights. Marriages and relationships have changed, in Western cultures. They are more 50-50 than 60-40, 70-30, 80-20, or 90-10. Some cultures have the wider-ratio relationships and men are the dominant sex. Women are put down and kept down. This does not work in Western society. Women see themselves as being equal to men, and that is that. More men have been accepting this ratio, especially the younger men but also quite a few of the older men. Women have equal say in any relationship with a man, which would include at work, home, on the street, and even on the telephone. They are not subservient. They make as many decisions. They have overall equality. Their ideas and contributions are equally considered and accepted. It is the better, more useable ideas/contributions that come to the front, and they aren't, necessarily, the man's, anymore. In years gone by, it had been the man's views that were considered to be the more important. It had almost always been the man's, when it came to the bigger decisions. Women's views were heard, or, at least, woman had some input, which is very different from having equal say.

Women now have rights and they are exerting their rights. Sexism can now whittle away at a relationship. You never know when or where it is going to show up, but it has a way of doing so, which is why it has to be defined and studied so it can be detected. It is an attitude—one of superiority. Sometimes, in a relationship, one person does become more dominant. One person may make most or all the bigger decisions. If the other person doesn't mind, this may be all right, but it isn't all right if the person who makes the decisions does not see and accept the other person as being equal and a full and contributing partner in the relationship.

Some couples are set up so one person is dominant and makes more decisions, and that person can be the male or the female. In such relationships, both should feel as if they are seen as being equals, and this is the whole point. In a free society, each couple has the right to live and be the way they see fit as a couple, but if the two people do not see themselves as being equal, with the potential and the space for having equal say and importance, then there is no legitimate equality and there will be discord. Equality can be of pretense. It may not really be there and it needs to be there so both can grow and develop and become whole. Otherwise, they will be stunted. Not all people are open to the idea of equality within relationships. Again, it is an attitude. Sexism needs to be rooted or booted out, wherever it is found. It will lead to problems. Both people in a relationship have worth and are growing— personally, socially, and culturally.

Today, there is relationship variance. Some are bisexual. Some are gay, or homosexual/lesbian. Regardless of the relationship type, there can be no sexism. Sexism can take on many forms. There are certain differences between men and women, but those differences have nothing to do with looking at a relationship as being 50-50 and giving equal regard and place to the other person in the relationship.

A small number of people prefer a same-sex relationship, and so lesbianism or homosexuality becomes their sexual preference. We are being thrust into a world where sexual relationships are diverse and not what they once were. AIDS has caused a societal shift in that sexual promiscuity has decreased because people are afraid of getting the disease, which is spread by a virus. Because people in the general population are afraid of getting AIDS, they find someone to pair up with as soon as they can, but, then they'll stop looking for someone who is perhaps more suited to them, because they have a relationship already. Even though the relationship may not really be what they want or may not be the best relationship for them to be in, they stop looking and may not be all that happy. Eventually, it catches up with them, and pressure forces them out of the relationship. Or, they stay in and they get too old, really, to find another partner. The older a person gets, the harder it becomes to find a partner to settle in with. One PBS series, *Vicious* (2013-2016), centers on two older gay men and the series somewhat covers the subject just noted.

Some people, today, require that an actual AIDS test be done before they will start a physical relationship with someone. An AIDS test is inexpensive and does not take that much time. A test for all STDs is sometimes done, as well. There have been people who knew they had AIDS but still engaged in sex with one or more partners, who had not known about the AIDS. Some people who are more sexually active have AIDS tests at many a bend and turn, but this is for their own peace of mind, not so much out of concern for other people. If they do end out harboring the virus, they have to try to figure out who gave it to them (and who they may have given it to).

Wasting time with someone not really right for someone (and losing some good years, really) is an awful dilemma to be in. Too often, the wrong person is picked as a partner and as a spouse, primarily because of sex. Not really getting to know someone can end out being disastrous, and traumatic. It can even sour people on re-marriage, after a separation or divorce. <u>This has become a national dilemma and such marriages are causing marriage statistics to go way down and the dilemma keeps creating more divorces.</u> Marriage statistics are down for other reasons, too. For one thing, people are afraid that they won't have enough money if they get married. Money is hard to come by, these days. It is hard to hold on to. Everyone and everything has tightened up, financially.

Some people join up or get married because of money. They believe they will be more financially secure with combined earnings. This can be good, or it can be bad. People constantly worry that they will run out of money or that there will not be enough (sooner or later). This is why there are at least some of the same-sex relationships, too. Same-sex relationships have increased because of fears about money.

Because of different fears, people are going in many directions, sexually. What people prefer sexually and who they prefer sexually is individual and it corresponds with the increase of new and varied ideas that have come into our society and world, particularly since the 1970's. It, so often, will correspond to money availability and to the economy—much more than is sometimes realized. Happiness is hard to find, though, and it is hard to hold on to or keep. People want love and they want to be happy and it just doesn't always happen for them. Of course, there are some people who don't apply themselves and get out and meet people so they can pair up with someone, but that is another issue, entirely. I will add, though, that it's not always easy to find a like-partner. It can be trial-and-error and exasperating, but you have to go to places where people have commonalities and similarities to you, if you are seeking someone. Don't go at it in a random, 'hit-and-miss' way.

It is best to start off only as friends and keep it that way, for a while. That way, you will give the other person plenty of time to decide if they really do like you enough to go to the next level. You will see more into the relationship and get to know the other person better. There are Internet Dating sites people click on to, and they meet people this way, too. There are group gatherings that are designed for mingling so a person can select possible dates, and then go on a first date. One type uses chairs, and everyone keeps changing chairs as they talk.

Many people are confused about the sexual permissiveness going on today. They may have certain, established values. They try this and they try that, and they even defend things that they really do not believe in and that they believe, down deep, are wrong. They allow themselves to be misled because some of society accepts that these things are around and so they allow themselves to agree with certain of these notions and practices. Reluctant people get pressured, then, to accept certain notions and practices, but in their heart of hearts, they believe that certain things are not right or best and that they fall short of their higher standard. They become very conflicted individuals. For one thing, there is a great deal of unfaithfulness that goes on in today's world, and they see it all around. They may believe that faithfulness in a relationship is an ideal, and important.

People who are going from one notion and practice to another—experimenting—and who are forming inconsistent values within themselves and passing this along to others, can be living anywhere in the world. At a given time, they may feel one way about something, then the situation changes for them and something new or different comes along that conflicts with former things. People go with the flow more than they should. They do not hold to a foundation of belief. They decide to do whatever is fun, alluring, easiest, most available, and what feels good. They do some things that may 'seem' right, even though those things may not be right to do. Some people will do what is most convenient or most satisfying, without having any consistent values or principles that they base their decisions on. Some theologians would say that many go 'the way of the flesh'. Not all people live inconsistently, but enough do that such chaos become evident. They are dominated by what looks, tastes, smells, and feels good. You can really become aware of this when you watch some of the talk shows, or even some of the court shows. Some people are governed by sexual desire, and common sense goes out the window. It can all be alluring and deceptive because some people just are not thinking straight. A number of people don't want to think straight, even when things are made clear. There are some people, however, who choose to abstain from sex until they are married. Some will do so until they meet 'the right person'. At times, this can be easier said than done but some have done this. They won't allow themselves to be in certain situations.

Most people are looking for the most stable road possible and they want to have a stable and normal life, but many are prevented from finding and having this kind of life for various reasons—one being that they can be in conflict with themselves because they haven't yet come to grips with their own values and beliefs. Their lives can become erratic and meaningless. The inconsistency around them and in their own life makes life very difficult for them to comprehend, and they end out doing what seems to be the easiest and the most gratifying. They do what seems popular, too, because they want to be accepted. They rationalize that what they are thinking and doing is all-right and they will become disagreeable if what they are doing wrong is pointed out. To some extent, though, and on one level and at times, it is all-right to go with what is easiest and most gratifying. The coin has two sides. You can only go that route at certain times, though. Today, everyone must proceed with caution.

In large groups, there can be peer pressure. In small groups, there can be peer pressure. A peer is anyone who influences a person and whose opinion matters to that person. There can be several peers in one's life. A peer is someone you usually have things in common with. You feel a bond with that person. Actually, there can be several bonds that tie you together. Peers can also put a collective pressure on a person, so all people must be careful who their peers are, in the first place. Still and all, a person should be generally independent from their peers, and they should think for themselves.

People who know what they believe and why they believe it, and who consistently act in accordance with their own beliefs, are happier, more secure, and more confident than people who haven't reached that place in life. Age doesn't seem to matter, at least to a point, except that younger people have had less time to process what they've been exposed to and have experienced in life. In fact, young people can be very confused. So can older people, though, especially if they haven't had the time or taken the time out to think or work through certain issues and ideas. Everybody has gaps. Many people need counseling because they are confused. There is a chapter about counseling at the end of the book. Even real old people need counseling, but some of them may be too proud to admit it. Older people are prone to get set in their ways and this can be a good thing or a bad thing, depending on each isolated situation, and belief.

When it comes to holding on to a marriage, it is important for people to find the best counselor possible if their marriage seems to be too weak. Look for an integrated counselor. Professionals who are working in a counseling capacity should determine their own values, sift out wrong values in their own personal lives, and become integrated individuals first, or they won't be able to counsel others effectively and be of much help to clients. Counselors need to have a firm foundation; otherwise, there won't be stability in the counseling sessions. Everything will be wishy-washy and will meander too much. But, at the same time, a counselor has to respect the rights of their clients, and allow their clients to think as they are able to or like they wish to think. They can then better guide their clients. A person may have to change counselors; such change is done by some. Some will even return to a previous counselor.

Look for a counselor who seems to have it all together. Sexuality and sex life are areas that all counselors and therapists encounter from time to time. The overall subject has many facets to it. Some counselors steer clear of sexuality and sex life; others delve into it; then, there are all those in-between. There are also actual sex therapists around and these professionals specialize in these areas. Some do not have certificates or college degrees, however, and so, too, with certain counselors. Even if there is a certificate (versus a degree), the certificate might be a weak one. They sometimes are. A college degree is always strong and authentic, except that some that can be achieved via the Internet may not be as strong as those achieved 'in person', while the person regularly attends actual classes in one or more tangible physical buildings. Some Internet sites are just diploma mills and it is too easy to get a certificate or even a diploma. Some can be good, but some are not.

Internet-college is essentially a correspondence program, which means limited experience and less ingraining of content, overall. There is no related classroom experience, which is what you get with campus-college. There are other lacks with such Internet programs, as well. It's just not the same as college/university attendance and experience. You set your own pace with Internet coursework. You cannot do that with campus-college or university. In any event, it is always a good idea to see a couple of diplomas on the wall of wherever it is that you choose to go to for any counseling. Give any counselor fair chance. You may need to go several times before you feel good about continuing with them.

# *Chapter 2*

# Detrimental Sex

The goal of most people is to have satisfying sex lives, to function well during sex, to be free from sexual hang-ups and restrictions, and to exercise sexuality in a way that they are comfortable with. Unfortunately, many people have one problem or another in these areas, often at different times during their life but sometimes straight through their life. Some people have very pathetic problems and seem to be helpless, quite frankly. Their lives are sad. A counselor has to help clients find a way through their problems and help them with their problems. Some situations are extremely delicate. All problems can be worked through or can, at least, become more minimal. Sometimes, there has to be attitude change.

Some people have problems that they create for themselves, and they either can't see something about themselves, or they don't want to see that something and so they won't. Others, however, have problems that are created for them and that are put upon them, by unkind, insensitive people, or simply by life's circumstances. It is easy to say "oh that person should have removed themselves from the situation", but maybe the person had too many external pressures on them that forced them to stay in the situation. They may have even been helpless to do anything about the situation. Many people have quagmire lives. They can still be helped. Sometimes even just talking about things can be helpful.

Some of sexuality is deviant or abnormal. In some cases, what is deviant or abnormal is subjective, but in other cases, certain sex practices and activities are believed to be deviant or abnormal by the majority within a society. Such sex practices and activities are usually criminal ones, and the criminals are called perpetrators or perps if a sex crime is committed or perpetrated on another person, of any age. Rape and child molestation are but two of these deviant crimes. In two other of my books, I cover sex crimes (along with other crimes). These two books are *Crimes, Crime Awareness, and Crime Prevention—Crime-orama Odyssey,* and

*Crime and Rehabilitation (Introducing the Gap Theory for Mental Assessment and Treatment.*

Sex that hurts another person is deviant and abnormal. That is a simple definition, but it is a fairly accurate one. For example, rape occurs when someone forces someone else to have sex when the other person doesn't want to have sex. The perpetrator rapes by either using real force or by intimidating or frightening the victim into giving in. Also, slipping in a date-rape drug or Quaaludes or any narcotic into someone's drink and then having sex with the person is considered rape. As another example, pornography includes porn images or pictures and these images or pictures can be a type of overkill because they overly excite or stimulate people into wanting to engage in sex. Unfortunately, some pornography includes rather rough sexual games and other pornography includes cruelty (and therefore causes confusion about the energetic side of lovemaking). Someone can actually be hurt by the rough play or by the type of activities that occur because of exposure to pornography. During the time when these kinds of sexual activities take place, harm can be done. The more sadistic type of pornography may incite unbalanced individuals to commit sex crimes. Any type of pornography can incite individuals to commit sex crimes, though—even the less-pronounced pornography can.

The ideal is to love the other person so much that you want to give yourself, sexually, to the other person, and so you do. Outside stimuli should be quite minimal, if at all. People can get stimulated without certain types of outside stimuli. They've been doing that since the days of Adam and Eve. Touching works, for example.

Pornography can stay in the minds of those who watch it so they will want sex more frequently and will want it when they want it. Pornography puts this pressure on people and it can become a controlling taskmaster. Some people can become obsessed with pornography and with sex. It becomes a controlling external. It can be a controlling nuisance, really, because it can put people into excess and into having sex for wrong reasons and into having sex when they shouldn't be having sex. Pornography breeds excess. It can cause people to have sex with someone who is not right for them. It has a way of insulting intelligence. People can, literally, become sex addicts, and they can, more readily, turn to committing sex crimes, even on their own spouse or partner and even on their own children. Sex films and books and magazines are only legally allowed to go up to a certain point, relative to what is shown or printed; past that point and they are going against the law—in large part because it feeds into criminal activity. Much pornography is banned but people can still get ahold of it. It's in people's homes. Sometimes the kids find it and watch it or turn all the pages. Then, they put it back where they found it and the parents don't even know they saw it. In many cases, it may only be one parent who knows about the porn.

Sad to say that whatever is seen in hard-core pornographic material can also be taking place in real life. For example, sadomasochism actually does occur between two consenting adults. It's not that common, but it does exist. You see it referenced or shown in film from time to time (for the shock value and ratings) but it is not as prevalent as you'd think. The urge to dominate and submit causes these things to go on, and sex can get way off balance. (The urge to dominate is the more common urge.) Whereas sadism demonstrates a desire to punish or hurt, masochism demonstrates a desire to be punished or hurt. Either situation is deviant and not in the normal range of behavior. Some people have sadomasochistic relationships, where one person controls the other person in an oppressive way. This gets carried out in the bedroom. There is psychological sadomasochism and there is physical sadomasochism. Neither is accepted in society, but it goes on. It tends to be secreted. Such a relationship is grossly unhealthy—short term and long term. No one should be in support of such relationships, let alone get into one like it. Genuine love cannot be present when such a relationship is present. Such a relationship is like slavery.

Another deviant sex proclivity is directed towards children. Clearly, kiddy porn or child pornography is to the far extreme of deviancy, especially when it creates pedophiles (and it does). The psychopath who preys on children must obviously be kept from doing harm to children. Such psychopaths wear an invisible millstone around their neck and society is quick to prosecute them and does not take such cruelty and actions lightly. Sometimes stepfathers and even fathers are pedophiles in their own homes, creating a prison of no escape for the children they prey upon.

Unfortunately, the computer has been used by pedophiles to get victims, but the computer has also been used to find out who these people are so they can be prosecuted. In 2002, the computer contents (of child pornography) found on David Westerfield's computer helped to prove his guilt. He had abducted, harmed, and killed a seven year-old child (Danielle Van Dam). (Sadly, he is but one of many who have abducted a child, sexually abused them, and then killed them.) Many a computer has been seized since that time, and computer and laptop evidence has been used to convict the guilty (or to free the innocent). Since the computer came into being, it has been used to trace many criminals, in all crime arenas. Child pornography is being fought by law enforcement, but it still keeps cropping up. People who peddle it, or who buy it, are prosecuted, and they are not well treated in prison.

Child abuse can occur sexually, in families, and it is being more exposed, these days. It used to be much more secreted. The abusing can occur in any type of home but the tendency is for it to occur in homes that are lower in income, and, of course, it is almost always perpetuated by men. It has occurred in homes where there are higher incomes, however, and even in homes where there are very high incomes. It's just less common in those homes. Young daughters are the victims and this can range from one daughter to all daughters in the home. Any in-home sex abuse and rape can be done by a father, an uncle, a brother, a business associate (to a parent), a friend of someone in the family, and even by a grandfather. Rarely does a mother participate in this kind of crime. The crime can happen once or it can happen several times. It can occur on a regular basis. It can even go on for years.

If a father is the abuser, he can be any age, even somewhat elderly. So often, there is at least some pornography involved on the part of the perpetrator. It could even be a milder form of it—like viewing bare-breasted women on pages. Sometimes, if it is a father, the father is not having a satisfying sexual relationship with his wife or is not having a sexual relationship with her, at all. Whatever are his reasons, and there could be many, it usually starts off by his sneaking into the child's bedroom when everyone else is asleep or when only the two of them happen to be home. He may, subsequently, give the child extra gifts or treats. He may threaten the child in some way so she won't talk. The child becomes frightened, confused, and depressed. The sex has to hurt because she is not full-size, unless the victim is a teenager and therefore larger. Also realize that the father is forcing the child or teenager to commit incest, which is an additional crime. Incest can occur with other male family members too, and the child is helpless to prevent it.

Child abuse is a perversion, no matter what. The perpetrator's mind is twisted and demented. It is quite a vile crime, and it is not tolerated. No man or boy has the right to do that to a young innocent child. Everyone is periodically reminded of some of these cases. Many children were abducted and abused, then murdered so they would not be able to identify the perpetrator, or they were murdered just for the sake of murdering someone. Child pornography can end out causing such deplorable crimes. Anyone who makes money off of child pornography is anathema (accursed).

Sometimes the wife gets wind of the sexual abuse that is going on in the home. A few will turn a deaf ear and pretend it isn't so. The wife may confront her husband and get lies in return. The child may or may not open up to the mother. The child may be too afraid to say anything. If the child does open up, and the wife (and mother) doesn't yet know about it, the child might not be believed and could even be scorned, which adds to the misery of the child. (Again, it can be a teenager that is being abused.) Such abuse leaves long-term mental scars and will mess up any child's, or teenager's mind and thinking. It is ingrained in society to help and protect children and young people, not hurt them, so people are repulsed by child sex abuse and rape.

Why people commit deviant sex acts, in general, usually has to do with the deviant's desire to control or to get back at society, or to get back at certain, specific people who are in society. Deviants don't always like to admit to that, but it is, so often, true. Sex can be used for good or for evil, and deviants have a distorted sense of their sexuality and of sex, in general. They don't just make one choice, either. They make a series of choices that are to the negative and are detrimental to society. Deviants can be helped, and some professionals don't like the word, deviant, but when there is a deviation from the norm, there is deviancy.

Voyeurism and exhibitionism is unusual and also deviant and it can cause harm that is different from physical harm. The harm is of a psychological nature, although it should be noted that anything causing physical harm naturally causes psychological harm, as well. Voyeurs and exhibitionists are almost always men. Oftentimes, these types of men (or perps) send obscene letters. They make obscene phone calls, too, or they used to until people got caller ID so that caller's names and phone numbers show up printed when anyone calls. These types can be any age, too, which goes to show you that older men can be as disturbed as younger men. Sometimes, they're even more disturbed, and deranged. These kinds of crimes are also power plays against women. These men want dominance and control. Some of them don't like women. In this day and age, with women being empowered, these men sense that they are spinning their wheels. Some men despise seeing women being empowered, but many of them will not admit this. Good men accept the equality.

Many of these types (voyeurs and exhibitionists) can become rapists eventually, although some never do. Whereas the one looks and peeks at what another has (the voyeur), the other displays what he has (the exhibitionist). The voyeur scouts for people who are nude or semi-nude, usually in their own home, but they can frequent nudist beaches and nudist colonies, too. Not everyone at these places is inclined to be this way, only a few are. They likely give the other nudists a creepy feeling, because they are creepy. The exhibitionist shows his nudity to others—back and/or front. They may have a coat on, for example, and then suddenly open it, in front of females. This is known as flashing. A streaker can run through an area while being naked but usually does this on a dare; a streaker flaunts common decency but may do this only one or two times. This person is not the kind of criminal the other is. Usually, streaking is almost always done when someone has been drinking. An individual's exhibitions are usually chronic (until they get caught).

Another type of exhibitionist is quite annoying to the public—to both men and women. A man (usually young) will openly fondle himself in rather private areas, which is a type of pornography, when you think about it. They will especially do this when women are around. They have some mental screws that are loose. In one way, too, it could be considered to be an act of hatred (towards women) because such men usually have no respect for women. Today, more crimes are being added to the hate-crime laws.

With the voyeur and the exhibitionist, the deviant is sexually stimulated by the act. Often, the exhibitionist will pick very young women as his victim because he believes that someone that young will be shocked by the act and not know what to do about it. They think that a younger woman won't bother calling the police. They want to shock the girl or woman, and when they do, it's a type of cruelty and usually these men very well know this. Therefore, there is some sadism associated with the exhibitionism. There is also sadism associated with voyeurism because often these men are misogynists and they have a hatred for women. They wish harm upon the women they view and that is why many voyeurs become rapists, and worse. Many voyeurs are rapists to begin with; they are at a window to check and see if they can break in, for example.

Voyeurs are also called Peeping Toms, and exhibitionists are sometimes called Flashers (since they can quickly open a coat and then close it), but some exhibitionists want to be seen a lot longer than just in a flash. It is usually men who do these things and again, these actions and maneuvers are usually a power play against women. Some men will sit with their penis out and play with themselves, knowing they are visible to others, especially to women. They're really the only one in the area who finds the activity erotic because onlookers are disgusted and get in contact with the authorities right away. Nowadays, people have cellphones and smartphones on them so they call the authorities right away. Today, an onlooker can even take a picture of such an exhibitionist so he will be bound for jail for sure. Consequently, there are now fewer of these deviants that are seen, but that doesn't mean that they aren't still around and would do such things if they could get away with it.

Women can become off-balanced sexually if they are a victim of these kinds of crimes committed by such miscreants. They can become repressed and think that something is wrong with sex. This can especially happen if a woman has been raped and treated very badly. Voyeurism and exhibitionism are nuisance offenses, actually, but they're crimes against society and against the State. These acts are 'control' acts. The Peeping Tom goes around looking into windows, hoping to see women undressing or scantily dressed. He thinks he has got one over on the woman (and society) if he sees her this way. He has invaded her privacy and space and has gained a negative control over the woman and society. It's really an artificial control because it is deviant. Some of these deviants break into homes and steal female underwear, which can be very intimidating for any residents in the home. Often, though, the woman lives alone or lives with one or more young child. Secretly, this thief really wants to control the woman by using fear because this kind of theft will frighten a woman.

More often than not, a man who is caught as a Peeping Tom had rape intent. He was looking through a window because he really wanted to rape the woman who lived there. He may have seen the woman somewhere before and followed her home, then chose a time at night for viewing, which was going to lead to an actual attack. Sometimes, the viewing is just to see if she is home so he can get into her home and rape her—then, or sometimes later. Therefore, he was not a Peeping Tom, per se. Perhaps he was looking for any woman in the area and he just happened to choose the one he did and hadn't seen her previously. Or, he could have been stalking one particular woman and she knows him by sight. Worse still, such men could be serial killers who happen to get caught peeping in a window before they are able to do something violent. All they get booked for is voyeurism, however (but police are wise to these guys). A few voyeurs (who are really casers) end out being thieves or burglars who scout or case out to see who lives where and to learn about an occupant's comings and goings. They aren't really looking for nude women or women to rape. Police keep a very close watch on any voyeur or caser who has ever been arrested. They know that different motives can be involved. For obvious reasons, Peeping Toms get booked for trespassing, too, and not just for the crime of looking into windows.

Sometimes Peeping Toms use binoculars to look into windows from a distance, and they aren't watching the birds or the stars. If there aren't good curtains, drapes, or blinds and they aren't pulled or shut, women (and sometimes men) are vulnerable to being seen (even in the privacy of their own home). Men generally aren't Peeping Toms with other men, though Women don't usually peep in at men when men are in their home. There are no Peeping Janes to speak of because women do not generally do such things, and they do not rape men. They're smaller and less muscular than men are, but there are other, more obvious reasons why women don't rape men.

Then there is the call girl or prostitute. The question is, is prostitution hurting anybody? And the answer is, yes, it hurts the prostitute because she (or he, as the case may be) is having sex with a large number of people without really caring for or about them. It hurts the wives of the husbands that go to prostitutes, too. For one thing, the money drains the family pocketbook, and for another thing, the hurt a woman experiences if she finds out that her husband has been going to prostitutes can be profound. The fact that a prostitute is available for single or married men makes it so that men don't feel that they need to try hard (or try at all) to find a marriageable mate, if they are single, or, to work at their marriage or stay married, if they are married. It decreases men's desire to work out certain of the problems in the relationship or the married life. Their own lives become artificial and phony, as well as off-center. They may be blind to this, or refuse to see it; meanwhile, the woman is suffering, unhappy, and is actually being belittled. The woman becomes back seat instead of front seat.

It is rare that any man can ever have a real relationship with a prostitute (one that lasts), despite what was outlined in the movie, *Pretty Woman*. Most prostitute patrons have little respect for prostitutes and they are unable to reverse that attitude. (This can be conscious or unconscious.) Some patrons secretly hate prostitutes. Some serial killers have even sought out prostitutes, to kill them. It's not a respectable profession and it's a difficult way of life for women. Many of them get STDs, and AIDS. Many want out of the profession. Many were forced into it, in the first place. Still, men don't usually feel that sorry for prostitutes. A rare man will try to help them get out of it. (Thank God for them.) Some ministries focus in on doing this. Some prostitutes are happy to be in it, though, because of earnings. But, many prostitutes don't have anywhere else to go, or they don't think they do. Also, there are only so many outreaches available, similar to what you would find with skid row outreaches. There's not very many of those, either—for both men and women. When and if an opportunity to get out comes around, prostitutes can miss the boat.

A married man both cheats on his wife and the family when he goes to prostitutes for sex. The family budget gets reduced. A man who cheats on his wife is not being a team player within his family. He is hurting the marriage and the kids, if he has any. He is actually committing adultery (the marriage has become adulterated). Some women become mistresses to married men but some mistresses are so like prostitutes, without the label, that they may as well be prostitutes. Were it not for the man's provision, the wife would leave the adulterer were she to find out about it. To a large extent (but not in every case) mistresses are really playthings and they are almost always second to wives, if they are even put in second place. Usually, they're not even in a place. The man may tell them 'sweet nothings' so they can continue the charade, but it's all superficial and blank. Affairs are different. A woman who is having an affair with a man (and not getting money or assistance because of it) is not a mistress. Still, affairs also hurt a marriage. Any infidelity does.

Prostitution hurts society because it roundaboutly erodes the family. Prostitution also hurts society because many prostitutes need drugs, and because prostitutes make easy money (some of them do, anyway), they then have money to spend on drugs, which they keep on buying. Prostitutes get hooked on one type of drug or another (or on several types—whatever is available) and then they have no desire to stay away from the drug, or drugs. They become addicts. They, then, sell sex to anybody. Prostitutes have often given 'private diseases' to those they have sex with and some of these diseases are incurable. AIDS is, of course, the worst. Two people who are faithful to each other, inside of a marriage, need not be affected by, or worry about, these outside 'negatives' coming into their marriage and sphere.

# Chapter 3

## The Gay World

Being bisexual can hurt another person, too, so it can be seen as a detriment in that respect, at least by some. Here is how it can be detrimental—a wife can be very hurt because her husband is having an outside relationship with a man. Her life can be ruined if the man separates himself from her and she has to, then, be alone. One woman I know of committed suicide because this dilemma-situation had become a part of her life. Today, there are women who have relationships with other women, while still retaining a relationship with a man, so the dilemma-situation can go both ways. This kind of triangle-relationship, and any kind of triangle-relationship, causes an imbalance of need fulfillment in a relationship or a marriage, and it can cause jealously, hurt, incompleteness, guilt, disrespect, and disgust. What is truly spiritual gets put in a locked cabinet. If people in these kinds of relationships act like they are not affected, they are lying to or deceiving themselves.

Homosexuality is unusual because two people who are not anatomically made for each other are sexually gratifying each other. This includes for lesbians. When two people of the same sex get involved in gay sexuality, it can potentially stop them from finding a sex partner of the opposite sex who they can relate to and find sexual fulfillment with. In this way, some people think it is detrimental. It could be said that they are roundaboutly hurting society because somewhere out there is a person of the opposite sex that they could really match up with (even though they say there isn't or don't believe there is), so that unpaired-up person is then forced to end out matching up with the wrong person or doesn't even end out matching up with anyone. This can also apply if people believe there is only one perfect match out there for every person who is meant to be married. Some people hold to that belief, but others do not. Most, in fact, believe that there are many people out there that you can match up with. Most gay people don't think much about either premise or principle and are content being where they are. Still, they will try to find someone they can have a relationship with, and be happy with, just like everyone else does.

Some people, who hold to either premise or principle, believe that gay people are too impatient to wait for the right opposite-sex partner and to abstain from sex and that they simply want their own way, i.e. to have sex when they want it. There very well may be a good, opposite-sex partner out there for them, in other words, but gay-inclined people will sometimes prematurely give up on finding that partner. These people believe that gays get on the gay treadmill, and then they can't get off or don't want to get off because they worry that they won't find a good opposite-sex partner. Some gay men, though, are turned off by women. Some feel superior to women. Some don't like women because they think they are too temperamental and bossy. Some women don't like men, either. They've had disappointments with men.

Sadly, for unattached women, some gay men are misogynists and they look down on women. They would never admit to this but we know it is true. Some guys go gay because they have a dislike for women but they will not outwardly acknowledge this because they can't. They secretly think women are too hard to deal with, so they prefer being with another guy. Some women may, or may not have disappointed them. Sometimes men will exaggerate things, to justify their being gay. Still and all, no one ever knows a person well enough to judge them. How can anyone ever know about everyone's past experiences and their thoughts? You have to be very careful when, and about how you go about judging anyone. You can have a reserved opinion, but set aside any judging because a) a story might not be over and b) only a Higher Power is capable of assessing any and all situations. However, many do not believe in a judging Higher Power, only in a Higher Power.

Mostly, gays generally feel that they have had no choice when it comes to what they've become and they feel that circumstances closed in on them and forced them to become gay. To emphasize—no one can judge another person's journey, mainly because no one can know all details, factors, and pressures that have, over the course of a person's life, affected that person. Just because you may know a few details about a person doesn't mean you can be their judge. Like everyone else, gays must continue their journey; they must make choices at every bend and turn. Some may leave the gay life and leave it forever. Some may continue with it. Some may even go into it more full-scale. Life is a journey.

I've counseled gay men who wanted out of the gay lifestyle, and I've counseled gays who did not want to change, and through these people, I was able to conclude some of the points I am now making. Some gays become rather disagreeable and even hostile towards people who want them to discontinue their gay lifestyle. They perceive that their lives cannot be changed and that they are locked into being gay.

They are trying to be as happy as they can be, with someone they've chosen to love. They certainly don't like to be told they have been or are currently wrong. Life is hard enough for them. If you don't like what they are doing, about the most you can do is plant a seed but the seed may not take root and grow. Besides, it is legal to be gay. It is illegal to cross the line into gay bashing. That is illegal. It is not illegal to generally lodge an opinion, but you cannot be hateful. You shouldn't want to get into the hate zone. If you find yourself becoming harsh and critical, stop talking. Show love to gay people, if you disagree with them. You don't have to compromise your own beliefs, though.

One cross-dresser I came across was one of the happiest persons I've ever met because he perceived himself as being free. He cross-dressed because he was gay. (Not all cross-dressers do so because they are gay, however). At the time, the last thing he wanted to do was change. That was years ago. Later, he changed, and he dropped the cross-dressing but he continued to be gay. When someone is 'that' happy about their chosen lifestyle, they want to stay right where they are. Time may bring about a change in such a person's attitude or belief, or it may not. Presently, little to nothing can be done to change or alter some people's behavior and beliefs, but change could come about later. It doesn't always, though, clearly.

Everyone has free will, and there are freedoms and protective laws for gays. Gays are more protected now (as well they should be). No one should hate a person for their being gay. In fact, gay people probably need more love than other people do. For many gays, it is not easy to open up about being gay; some have even committed suicide because they could not overcome the disapproval that came their way after they'd bravely opened up about their sexuality. These gays needed love, and they didn't get enough of it when they needed it. This noted, there are many gays who should not be gay. They could go the other way. Why not be frank about that point? It isn't right that some gays become gay just because they hate society (or even hate, or fear, women). They could get over that, with counseling or with time. There are better, more substantial reasons for becoming gay, in other words. Many want to hurt society because society has hurt them. They turn on society. That is why some become gay. They want to be anti-social. This is not good. It is sad.

Society is second to some (not all) gay people's own wants, in that they don't care if they hurt some segments of society by doing what they are doing. And, what they are doing does hurt some segments of society—in some ways, anyway. Certainly, not all gays are inclined this way. Again, if a male is a homosexual, he is causing some woman out there to be single and without a partner. There are more homosexuals than lesbians. (There are more women than men in the world.) If a female is a lesbian, she is causing some man out there to be without a partner. The gay life can be looked at this way, but it generally isn't.

Choosing to be gay is gay people's business, of course, and legally they have the right to be gay and to live their one-time-around life any way they want. However, many straight people get upset if they think that gay people are trying to recruit young people into becoming gay, especially if those young people happen to be their own children, or other children that they know and feel protective towards. Other people do not care about such recruitment, one way or the other, but quite a few people really do. Gay people believe that their own lives are theirs and theirs alone and that they have the right to pursue happiness as they perceive happiness to be. Some people believe that recruiting is carrying that freedom too far.

Some gays are always going to be blatant and defiant about being gay. There will always be gay parades and marches. Some even want to throw being gay into people's faces, while others just want to make a statement. Some are, even, still in the closet. Others are out but keep a low profile about being gay. There are those who merely want to be honest and let people know they are gay. They are matter-of-fact about it and do not want to, or mean to rock any boat. Some aren't really against society and they aren't really anti-establishment, which is the better approach compared with throwing defiance around. Most gay people are sensitive, and are not so crass. There is a segment of gay people who are super kind and sensitive. They draw everyone to them and you like to be around them. Many gays have suffered emotional set-backs because of their being gay, and consequently, they are more sensitive to human suffering, and also to animal suffering. They are caring people.

Society is beginning to accept lesbianism and homosexuality more inclusively. In fact, quite a few people believe that the genuine lesbian female or homosexual male should not be classed as deviant. In other words, the behavior of gays is acceptable because it is an authentic expression of their nature, or of how they perceive their nature to be. Some see being gay as a medical issue. In fact, many do. Declared public sympathy is going out towards the lesbian and homosexual, more and more, because people believe that a number of gays aren't able to help their inclination and preferences and that they can't help the way they are and the way they are made. They were dealt a genetic hand of cards, and that is what they are permanently stuck with, in other words (or blessed with, as some might see it). Some gays believe they have a genetic predisposition to being gay, and so being gay is logically explained and justified, but all this far from applies to all gays. It only applies to some of them.

The genetic predisposition view is around, but there are still many who don't agree with it and they probably never will. The perspective is an educational and even researched viewpoint. Regardless of belief and outlook, it seems right that people should be accepted for the person they are, and not because they are gay or even straight. Gays need to accept straight people, too, and some of them really don't.

The other side of the genetic predisposition argument is that many gay people don't have such inclinations due to genetic predispositions. They just choose to be gay. It is what they want to do, not what they have to do. Again, some gay men dislike women and feel that women are inferior to men. Some gay men do not like to be around women, unless they have to be. This is so very sad but it is very true and informed people realize this can sometimes be the case. Because some gays had bad or unpleasant experiences with women (or they thought they did), they end out preferring the company of men. (This point also relates to women who become lesbians, only the two sexes are reversed.) Again, some gay men even believe women to be weak and inferior but, again, they can't admit this around others or there would be a backlash. There can be no discrimination against women, these days. We live in Me Too Movement times. Male chauvinism will always be around, and it can be found many places and in many situations.

To be fair and honest, some male assertion is justified and justifiable. Male assertion is not the same as male chauvinism, but it can be male chauvinism. Much depends on the circumstance and situation. (Some women have deserved some criticism.) So much depends on the outlook, though, of the particular male. What are his true values, in other words? When it comes to his view about women, a man might simply be competing and may see women in respectful ways. He may not be intending chauvinism. Still, there are insinceres and phonies out there and they think they are better than women and some of them devalue women. They do not wish to give any woman any space and those men are the true chauvinists. Today, they will keep such views very low profile and under wraps but they are there. Men and women are just different and have separate and unique attributes. Neither sex is superior. Both sexes are needed in this world and each contributes. Both sexes deserve to have equal rights and to be treated well.

Some nice looking, eligible bachelors go gay, to the chagrin of eligible bachelorettes or single women. It's very sad but today, some women end out being very lonely. As noted earlier, some gay women despise men, because too many men have let them down and this is why some women have turned to the gay way of life. Their being gay has nothing to do with genetic predisposition but it has everything to do with past experiences and environment. Even when a man, in a borderline way, looks a little effeminate, or a woman, in a borderline way, looks a little masculine, whereas in years gone by they found opposite-sex relationships and stayed with them, today, they might be prone to go gay. There was a time in society when even the somewhat effeminate men and the somewhat masculine women would always choose to be in a same-sex relationship, or they would end out in no relationship at all, but today, there seems to be more freedom to choose to be gay.

One problem, for women, is that there have been and are fewer men than women available for dating, and therefore, for marriage; consequently, more women are choosing to become lesbian. Or, they choose to stay single and live as a single. Again, quite a few women are upset that male gays have been increasing in number because they feel that there are now less men available for the marriage market. When two men are coupled, that means <u>two</u> men are off the market. They may not say that they are, but they are. This can become very depressing for women of any age. It genuinely depresses women. It causes a bit of a panic for women. When fewer men are in the marriage market for them, their odds of being married are reduced. This has been becoming an increasing problem, and has affected population increase.

Gay marriages have been increasing considerably since the turn of the Century. Many new laws went into effect, in a number of USA states. Gay marriage was also accepted in several other countries, besides the USA. The advantage for gay people who marry is that they have inheritance rights. They can combine their incomes under one roof. Other legal matters will be in their favor. There are also civil partnerships, legally set up in certain areas. This is the next best legal document gays can secure, aside from a marriage certificate.

It is somewhat sad because more gay men get married than gay women. The more (gay) men that aren't available to a person of the opposite sex, then that means that more women who are looking for a male partner will have to be alone. Single women look around and get discouraged and even depressed when they see slim pickings, which is sometimes the case. At some point, women may even panic if they sense they are not going to be able to find a life partner. Women today are sometimes worried that someone they're interested in could be gay. Some are afraid to date. It's very sad. Women have to ask a lot of questions, these days.

Terms began to be added to the gay world after the Millennium (year 2000), too, and now, the overall gay world is given the abbreviation LGBT (and sometimes, LGBTQ). These abbreviations stand for Lesbian, Gay, Bisexual, Transgender, and Queer. The word, queer, used to be used pejoratively, but now, it is not. I do not know why the group of letters starts with an L, nor why there is no H present, for Homosexual. You'd think it would be LHGBT. Lesbian implies Gay so why not forget the Gay and add in Homosexual? And why even put in the Q part, for Queer, when using the five letters versus the four? Who, specifically, identifies themselves with the word, queer, these days? It means odd or unusual. Apparently some people do. Most people go with the four-letter identification of LGBT and the letters refer to the grouping, as a community. LGBT people wish to be referred to as a community. They started to become more of a political force as soon as they were labelled a community. This time period was around 2015 to 2020. They have always been political, though, but they weren't very organized for years.

You didn't start to hear about gay people until the AIDS scare came around. There didn't used to be very many gays around, not until Rock Hudson was forced to come out because of AIDS. Pre-Rock Hudson, and there just weren't very many homosexuals or lesbians. There were a few in California, and a few around New York but they tended to be closeted. When drugs entered the USA and other countries during Viet Nam days, and thereafter, young men started to 'go gay' but it took a while before there were very many gays. By the 1990s, there were quite a few gay people and Gay Rights increased considerably during the 1990s. Before then, it was not that much of a movement. Some like to say it was, but it wasn't. Too many were still closeted and kept a very low profile, and there were not that many gay people, in the first place.

There was absolutely no marching in the 1960s or 1970s for Gay Rights. Some are saying there was, but no, there wasn't. Maybe some small group somewhere, like in New York, may have gathered for a small protest, but nothing on a large scale was ever a part of any protest for or on behalf of Gay Rights. You didn't, really, see this until the 1990s (and somewhat in the 1980s because of all the AIDS deaths). Even in the 1980s, Gay Rights was not a formalized movement so there weren't marches and protests. A few more people were becoming gay, but nothing was much approved of or sanctioned by the bulk of society. There was still opposition to what was gay, generally. I was socializing a lot during those years and in touch with many people. I was in the schools and I did some counseling and I remember all the trends.

There were only two areas that brought about mass marches and protests—Civil Rights, and the Viet Nam War. Women's Rights were in the front, too, but it was much more gradual and even background with that Movement and was never as heavy-weighing as either Civil Rights or Viet Nam was. The Women's Movement has been slow and steady and continuous. It is still going on (slowly but continually). There was an Environmental Movement, too, mainly from the 1970s reference clean air and water, but there was no Global Warming Reversal Movement. Since the 1970s, Civil Rights has been huge. You wouldn't think it has been because of certain goings on in 2020, but they have been huge. Women's Rights have been steadily accumulated. This has somewhat been the trend with Gay Rights, too.

Laws in the area of Civil Rights and Women's Rights have been passed, all along the way. Because so many laws have been passed in the arenas of both Movements, you could, perhaps, conclude that both Movements have peaked. It doesn't seem like they have peaked, but on one level, they have. The Rights are now right, in other words. They are set in motion and in stone. Some issues are still being worked out that center on passed laws, but the foundational and basic laws have been passed.

Gay Rights laws have been passed, too. The Movement may not have reached its peak, though, and will it, ever? It differs from Civil Rights and Women's Rights. It differs because religious America, in the main, sees rights for minorities and for women as being religious-based, but many in religious America do not see Gay Rights as being religious-based. Some do, but many will not change their religious views, or even the medical-related views centering on Anatomy and sex and reproduction. Really religious people would go so far as to love and accept gay people, but they would not cross the line and accept what they are doing. There will be tolerance, but not acceptance concerning that one aspect of a gay person's life. It's not difficult to love a person but you do not have to accept everything they believe in or stand for. You should not hate or discriminate against anyone for any reason. Such discrimination days are long gone, really. We are so much more informed and civilized now.

There's been many good contributions made in the USA over many years. The acquiring of rights does not mean that one group that was awarded rights should be granted more rights and privileges than other groups. The acquiring of rights should not go to anyone's head . . . and it sometimes does. Rights are granted but they aren't granted at the expense of other groups of people—not in a structured and established Democracy. Some people lose sight of that and become over-inflated. Rights are shared, too. Other people have the same rights you have. So many laws have been passed over the years, and legislators will keep on passing them, when and as they are needed. Clashes here and there, anymore, are not so much because of a lack of rights, but because of a lack of money. All groups are clamoring for money and are at odds with other people because of money.

Many have been involved in the party politics of the Democrats but a few LGBT people are Republicans. They became political because gay rights became an issue that was supported by the Democratic Party. Because the Democrats got so many laws through for them, the Republicans began to follow general suit with the Democrats. No one wants to get in trouble with the ACLU, relative to people's civil or gender liberties.

Now that gay marriage is legal, more gay women are coming out. They can derive more benefits now, by living together. Some lesbians even adopt children together. They can obtain a child by finding a surrogate or one of the partners can have a baby by way of artificial insemination. Adopting children is less common with homosexuals and is a little harder to do, but a few gay men will do it. They, too, can go the way of a surrogate, if they have the money. Going the way of surrogacy is always risky, though, because the real mother can always change her mind.

There are, at least, some gay people who deceive themselves into thinking they have gay leanings or inclinations when they really could have easily chosen to take care of, and love a member of the opposite sex. They could have easily drawn in a member of the opposite sex, if they chose to do that, and they could have given that a go. Internet dating (and matching) could have helped them with that. Some gay people could have also gone celibate, instead of going gay, but they may have thought they would be depriving themselves if they became celibate. Therefore, they wouldn't have wanted to wait for a member of the opposite sex to come along when a same-sex partner may have been, more readily, available. Why put out the effort to find and love a member of the opposite sex and work at that relationship, in other words. (We'll go the easier route and go gay, in other words.)

People go to gay bars and parties where there is alcohol and drugs and they fall into becoming gay. People have the right to do that, though—by law. But again, it should not be external pressures that cause a person to become gay. Alcohol and drugs should have nothing to do with anything of such personal and social significance. A person has to decide to be gay on their own and be under no influence, whatsoever, when they do. They might change their mind, later on, based on new exposures, but they might not, too. They have a legal right to choose whatever sexual orientation they want. Younger people might want to give this decision more time. It is a big decision. Once you go down that road, it will become very difficult to get on a different road. You can get locked into it, like it or not.

There are some men and a few women who are caught between a rock and a hard place. They haven't yet decided anything. Again, there are far fewer lesbians than homosexuals. Some men are more effeminate and some women are more masculine. It is usually these people who think, much more so, about possibly going gay. Their lives can be altered or changed by behavior and also by mode of dress. It can certainly be changed by plastic surgery and often is, in this day and age. Again, some people choose to become trans-sexual and have medical and surgical operations. Some men, for example, may have had various problems while they were growing up, and as a result, psychological and deep-rooted feelings became a part of them and they really do have a psychological proclivity towards being gay and even transgender. It is the same with some women. But they could still work through these issues, if they wanted to bad enough. This would be their choice, though.

Some give effort to working through their issues but to no avail. Every gay person is different, and they are gay for different and sometimes very personal reasons. Outsiders and even some family members may not know what the real reasons are. Some people might even be surprised were they to learn some of the reasons. Some of their reasons might relate to practicality, on one or more level. Some reasons should generate compassion. There are some gays who may even be being forced to pimp themselves, because they lack money. The young man, Andrew Phillip Cunanan, who shot Johnny Versace in 1977, had been pimping himself, here and there, and he was desperate for money so he went to Johnny Versace's mansion, hoping to be taken in by him, but drugs had gotten to the young man, to an excess, and Johnny Versace did not want him in his home. Hence, the shooting, because of financial desperation and his feeling abandoned.

Gays do not deserve to be bashed or hated—far from it. They should be loved and treated well. Equal means 'the same'. Gays have equal rights to other people in society and so they should have equal position. Some gays are very popular, too, often because of their personalities. As noted earlier, gays tend to have an acquired sensitivity towards others, in large part because they've been through a lot, and have suffered, because of their conflicts and their identity issues. Certain gays have something going for themselves, in other words, because of this sensitivity. Some gays are very prominent men, in society. They have wealth. Not all of them come out, but more have been since around 1990 (some years back).

It's when something gets thrown in your face that people become irate. Gays should try to keep to decorum, and not flaunt their being gay in an obvious way, as some have done. No one likes to be around a show-off, especially if they're being smug and arrogant. It doesn't matter what the issue is all about, no one likes someone who ranks from a 7 to a 10 on the smug and arrogance scale. Always keep things at 5 or lower, is a good creedo. Be confident. Don't be arrogant. No one likes it when something is imposed on them, either, especially if they don't totally or, at all, agree with it. People like to decide things for themselves and on their own and in their own time. Realize that people can and do change, regardless of what the situation is. Minds can gradually change.

Still, many people are opposed to the social and legal situation about gay rights and they resent the fact that gays are increasing in number. They are projecting their worry to the time when their own children or grandchildren may be exposed to the gay life and when they may even be propositioned or invited to participate in gay sex. Sometimes, outlook changes in society are very slow to occur. On the surface they may seem changed, but basically, under the surface, society as a whole has not changed that much about this overall subject. It may seem like it has, but only on one level, it has. The older people are against the gay life, in general. The younger people aren't. Overall, though, there is more tolerance and acceptance these days towards gay people because of laws and also because of the principle of equality.

With some people, it isn't the gay people but the gay life, itself, which people are upset about. To add, no one likes seeing people being mistreated. Today, however, gays are extended rights and courtesies, just like everyone else is.

No one can discriminate against a person because of their sexual proclivities, orientation, or lifestyle. Some of the young people who used to think that this kind of discrimination was all right, do not think that way anymore (although, some still do.) Instead, they see gays as having equal rights like everyone else has and so they live and let live. Equal means equal and fair treatment, lest anyone forget. That's all there is to it. You cannot refuse to serve gays, even if they are seen holding hands, embracing, or kissing, which some are now doing in public. Some do this naturally and innocently but some are wanting to flaunt their being gay around other people. There is the notion of gay pride, which can be looked at differently by the different gays.

Sometimes parts of gay-rights history get distorted and misunderstood. Very little has really gone on until after the year 2000. Not much was all that 'open' and the movement was small and generally weak. It really wasn't even a movement. One milestone for the history was Rock Hudson's death. Rock Hudson was a much-loved actor who got AIDS and died from AIDS. Then, there was the case of young Ryan White, who got AIDS from a blood transfusion and died from AIDS, too.

AIDS caused people to be sympathetic towards people who got AIDS because it was a ravaging disease, which killed people. People started to feel sorry for gays with AIDS, and the subject of gay people was always before the mainstream so people were talking about all these subjects much more than ever before. Other notable people died from AIDS, too. Sometimes, AIDS wasn't put on the death certificate and something else was but people knew, or strongly suspected that the person had died from AIDS. Another actor, Robert Reed, died from AIDS, in 1992. He starred on *The Brady Bunch* television series. One celebrity who is believed to have died from AIDS was Amanda Blake who played Kitty Russell on the *Gunsmoke* television series, which ran for twenty years. She was Kitty the whole time. It is believed she contracted AIDS from a husband. She died at age 60. Quite a few celebrities have died from AIDS, and the public never found out about it. It was kept quiet. Some information about their death came out later. Sometimes, though, it never did.

There is a History of Gay Rights but it is being plummeted with occasional wrong details because some gays are so zealous about pushing for gay rights. They can get a little blinded and there has been some misrepresentation. For example, what some try to pass off as having been gay bars back in the 1960s really weren't gay bars. They were really just bars for street kids, in general. There were almost no gays in the 1950s, 1960s, and 1970s. There were a few but not many. Being gay was just too ostracized, and even laughed about, as if a joke. Most men scorned men who were gay. Women were never afraid to go out with men because men weren't gay and they could view men they dated as being a possible marriage partner. Some rowdy bars mostly got busted because of bootlegging, not because boys were gay. Liquor gets brought in from unlicensed places that are not, then, taxed. It gets brought in on the sneak. Liquor gets watered down, too, and prices for it end out being high. Sometimes, price regulations were violated at these bars so they got busted for that reason, too, and not because gays had been at those bars. People who film can make a bar (that wasn't a gay bar) look like it was exclusively a gay bar, when the bar was busted. There were no gay bars that far back. There weren't many gay people.

People who were around then claim they never knew any gays, ran into any, or even knew of any gays. It's not right that numbers or occurrences get exaggerated, yet they are, by some. There were just general bars, for anyone and everyone. Even street kids and delinquents back then weren't gay. They wanted girls or young women. I lived through those times. I read magazines, newspapers, and was in the know. I knew a lot of people—well. My parents were around then, too, and they don't remember any gays, nor does anyone I know. There were essentially nil, except for the very few closet ones…and I do mean, very few. That kind of consciousness was not, yet, around.

You can film what could be labelled a gay bar (but it really isn't) and can even film cops raiding it, but the cops might only be raiding it because too many under-age kids frequent the place or for other reasons, too, but not because4 it is a gay bar. However, the police back then did arrest homosexuals—the few there were—because it was not legal to be gay or to solicit other men for sex, which some men were suspected of doing and so gays encountered entrapment on occasion but there was essentially very little of that going on. Solicitations didn't start up in public bathrooms until much later. Gay proponents want you to think bathroom solicitations went on much sooner than they did and that there were gay bars much sooner than there were.

There truly were almost no lesbians from 1950 to about 1980 but even from 1980 to 2000, there weren't very many. You started seeing more after 2000 and especially after 2010. You can parallel these dates with homosexual history, too, although, there have always been more homosexuals than lesbians. Being gay is now legal. The setting and environment is different. <u>But, there have started to be historical errors and deceptions and this makes even the people who are all for gay rights angry</u>.

When history gets distorted and false applications get put on previous events and happenings and there is gross exaggeration and error, people who are in the corner of what is lawful will get upset and want the wrongs made right. People want the arrow to be shot straight. If being gay is legal, why does there have to be exaggeration and misrepresentation of times and occurrences? No distortion is even necessary. Just think about that. Be true to what has truly been the history. People see through the untruths, especially if they are older and were alive at the time. Some younger people are too gullible and should be more reserved and give some issues more time. The moral of the story is—you shouldn't always believe what is easiest to believe or what you want to believe or what you first hear. There are different ways of being dishonest. Not all dishonesty, or lack of truth, is intentional, but some of it is.

People are still vocal about what they think and believe about homosexuality and lesbianism, but it is at their own risk because they can be called gay bashers. Some have been arrested for being vocal, and have even been put in jail or prison for a hate crime. Everyone is free to choose a view or position (or to stay in the middle). America allows freedom of belief, and of speech, but there are limits and you cannot cross certain lines. For many, certain family and home values, and values about sex will always be held on to. A wide tolerance today about gay rights is going to continue because of the laws that protect gays. Laws that protect gays vary from state to state, if they aren't federal and uniform around the whole nation.

No matter how you feel about someone's lifestyle, you have to accept and sometimes even love the person, depending on your relationship with that person. Just because you accept and sometimes love a person who is gay does not mean you, yourself, have gay inclinations, but many people used to think that way. If someone even talked to a known homosexual, they could be ostracized by others. Hence, there was more of a taboo about someone being gay and more hostility toward gays, since they had absolutely no support, back in time. For some time, people did not want to identify with or be identified with gays, or with anyone who was even perceived of as being gay. They didn't want people to think that they, too, were gay. Today, people are more open-minded and understanding about these things. Everyone feels sorry for struggling people, and even today, life is not easy for gay people. All citizens have rights.

To emphasize, in 2015, The Supreme Court met on and voted that same-sex marriages were legal, which was quite a step forward for gays. In that same year, a well-known TV personality (on *Keeping Up with the Kardashians*) went very public about his turning transgender. This was, of course, Bruce Jenner, who subsequently became Caitlyn Jenner. Likely, he legally changed his name to Caitlyn, through the court. To become a woman, he had feminization plastic surgeries—quite a few of them, in fact—on both his face and body. All was covered by the media, big-time. She got her own reality show, *I Am Cait*, hoping to change public views about the transgender world. In the shows she presented, sympathy was shown to the transgender.

Bruce Jenner had been quite masculine, actually; he was even an Olympic Decathlon winner in 1976, winning the Gold. Bruce Jenner had also raced cars and was a motorcycle enthusiast. He seemed to be 'all man'. He'd been either a father or a step-father to ten children over the course of his life. Suddenly, he decided to become a woman. He had the money to do it. It pretty much shocked the world and continued to shock the world for some time. Not everyone thought it was a great move on the checkerboard, but he got plenty of lauding and encouragement. Some saw him as a hero. His family stuck with him for quite some time. Then, they all somewhat seemed to live their lives more separately.

Caitlyn (aka Bruce) Jenner wanted to help the transgender segment of society, and she did, because of all the media focus and the time that was given to her. Plus, much of her transitioning was shown on *Keeping Up with the Kardashians* show when it was on, and faithful viewers of that show, myself included, were able to get inside her mind and learn, at least, some of the whys that had centered on the transition. Her reality show (*I am Cait*) that was subsequent to these other appearances, had good ratings, as well, but it was cancelled not too long after it had started. Most people expected her to have sex organs modified, after one year of 'coming out'. By August of 2015, she had made a complete transition, aside from having any final sex organ surgeries. (It is rumored that these were eventually done.) She also began to embrace the gay community and went to their gatherings. In the end, she had more surgeries. Caitlyn Jenner never lacked company.

Caitlyn Jenner was given the Arthur Ashe Courage Award for 'coming out' and at the ceremony, she encouraged people to "accept people for who they are", which for some people is easier said than done. Not all accepted her collectivity of choices. The one choice brought on a chain reaction of other choices that she essentially had to make. Her family had mixed feelings about her choices. It took them some time to sort through it all. They are all good communicators, which helped. At some point, she could not go back.

In this world, it is laissez-faire and now the once-upon-a-time athletic man is referred to as she. Previously, as Bruce Jenner, Caitlyn Jenner had done many TV appearances—in sit-coms, infomercials, and game shows and from 1980 and on through the 2015 transition. He had done a number of advertisements. He'd been an actor in film, too; he had held his own quite well on the *Keeping Up with the Kardashians* reality show. Then, being experienced in film, she did her reality show as a woman, hoping to help transgender people. Any other motives Bruce Jenner may have had were known only to him. Many people around the world missed the old Bruce Jenner and had thought he had been pretty special. Bruce Jenner stated he had never been attracted to men and was exclusively only attracted to women— before the transition—but he also said this could change, in time. Bruce Jenner was 65 years old at the time of the onset of his transition. After the transition, her personal life became her own. By 2018, there was little to nothing on the News about her. The story faded out, as all big stories tend to do. Every so often, you would see her at events and gatherings that were featured on the News.

In part, Caitlyn Jenner went through the step-by-step process of transitioning with the intention of helping the group of young people who are betwixt-and-between finding their own identity but were confused about it. Some young people are struggling with their sexual identity. Certain young males may have feminine inclinations and certain young females may have masculine inclinations. When those inclinations seem to lean more heavily to the extreme, they are inclined to think of themselves more as the opposite sex than as their birth gender.

Caitlyn Jenner wanted to be there for these young people who have gender-identity issues. Those who are transgender are also older people. Some older people can be confused and marginalized and they also need some guidance or corroboration. When people perceive themselves as being different from the majority of those of their own birth gender, they struggle with it. They go back and forth about it until they no longer can. Some have struggled so much with gender identity and many have had personal acceptance problems. As noted before and to emphasize, the pain and stress it has all caused them even caused some of them to commit suicide. Suicide is a premature, too-early death. Many say, about their suicide, "if only they had given themselves more time". If pain, be it physical and/or mental, gets to be too much, people want to escape. If there are basic-need deprivations, people want to escape. Many who are transgender have difficulty in the work world because they are so different from mainstream society. This is a big reason why those who are transgender hesitate to go the transgender route. It adds to their pressure, considerably, all across the board. They have to work. They have to earn money. They have to be around people. This has been changing, though.

Today, because of people like Caitlyn Jenner, there is more acceptance of, or tolerance for people who have these more masculine or feminine attributes and when they are the opposite sex to what those masculine or feminine attributes and inclinations tend to be. Many gay people do not struggle with this physical issue, per se. They choose to be gay and do not have these opposite gender attributes, but for those who do have them, there is more help out there for them now, and more comfort and acceptance, as well. There is more understanding now, about their dilemma and the overall situation. Gender identity has become a part of sex education programs in schools, but much else is taught in these programs. Many parents do not like it being offered in the schools. There have been parent protests over the whole program or over parts of the program. Some parents are concerned that gender-identity changing could be pushed on their child or children. Many parents live within a Christian perspective. Gender identity changing will never be accepted by many people. Some parents have had to accept it. Some parents have willingly accepted it.

We have to teach aspects of sex education to young people in a wholesome way. Adolescents experience (for the first time) the full force of the sex drive. They have great curiosity about putting their sex drive into practice, and they also have anxiety about the psychological and physiological changes that they are experiencing. Adolescents worry about feelings they do not understand, have doubts about their own worthiness and attractiveness, and often find it difficult to talk about sex. They worry about how their parents will react to their feelings, and to their actions if their parents were to find out that they were having sex. Reticence or shyness leads to accident-proneness. The accidents range from inadvertent pregnancy and/or compulsive promiscuity, or to disabling shyness and numbness and guilt. Any of these outcomes can permanently handicap current and eventual personal relationships.

Sometimes, adolescents (and even children) can approach a school counselor about an issue regarding sex, if it relates to school in some way—directly or indirectly. School counselors hear about sex abuse, teen pregnancies, heartbreaks, stalking, gender confusions, and other issues and they are prepared to help resolve situations, even if it means contacting parents, or the authorities.

Values are usually projected into sex education for youth and this is where the controversies arise because few are against sex education, per se. Exact time for introduction of sex education can become an issue, though, and has, many a time. Sometimes sex education is introduced in elementary school, for example. These days, parents are paying closer attention to sex-education curriculum and too-early an introduction is one of the reasons why. Some parents don't like it. All parents should be concerned about this area of learning for their children and adolescents. If the process of emotional growth proceeds smoothly for a young person, he or she will achieve that integration of personality that we understand to be maturity. The individual who remains trapped at an earlier stage suffers from an arrested development. He or she can be emotionally stunted and may never grow up and may never grow up right. He or she will have gaps, which may or may not be obvious. I write extensively about these gaps in one of my books—*Crime and Rehabilitation*—and I use the words, gap and gaps, quite often in my writings.

Sex education, if it is in the schools, should contribute to preparing young people for future relationships and for marriage. That should be the main focus. It was the main focus, initially, but the focus has moved over to include some other goals and some of these goals sometimes get more focus. So many young people are having sex these days that pregnancy prevention (including contraception) and social diseases and AIDS prevention have been incorporated into sex education programs. Gender identity is also now given space, in sex-education programs. The question is, how much space should it be given?

# *Chapter 4*

# Marriage-Compatibility and Roles

Marriages will always be important and needed in society because we need stability in our society. We need families. Overall, people seem to be happier when they are in families. People like to be a part of something. We also need children, and children need the stability of a secure two-parent home (preferably and ideally). Some are not fortunate enough to have a two-parent home, and they have to go through life as best they can. Some end out doing very well anyway. However, some don't do very well. Many times, the mother ends out raising the children, and consistent male behavior, attitudes, and general ways are not witnessed or witnessed enough by the children. This can cause lopsidedness and several gaps. Also, women who have to work—sometimes two jobs—are not there much for their children. They can't be. They're too worn out when they are home. This can also cause a lopsidedness or some gaps. Household income may be less, too, which can create problems and lacks for the children. Children don't ask to be born, but many of them find themselves in these kinds of situations.

Singles differ from marrieds in that they do not have to be accountable to another person, at least not usually. They can do more of what they want to do when they want to do it, or so it may seem. But actually, marrieds, if they are working towards joint goals and have a happy, relatively tension-free and co-operative relationship, and if they have an adequate degree of compatibility, can end out doing what they want to do when they want to do it, and this would include in the area of sex because they are able to have sex with each other whenever they want too. In fact, marrieds have sex much more often than singles do. Sex can relieve life's tensions, and can add an element of happiness to the lives of both partners in a marriage. That feeling of loneliness that singles often have is greatly reduced or is nonexistent for people who are married.

Singles need to make sure, if they are about to marry, that sex is not the carrot at the end of the stick; rather, they must be certain that they have a deep love for the other person and that they have a secure feeling within themselves that they are doing what is best for the two of them together, as a couple, and for each one of them, separately. Before going into a marriage, people need to have a strong sense that the marriage will make their lives better. It is always best to have at least some counseling—both together and separately—before getting married or tying the knot. Ideally, that knot should never be untied, but we all know that it oftentimes is.

Most people marry, and sometimes more than once. Transitioning into marriage from single life does not mean that a person can keep their old boyfriends or girlfriends, or previous partners around. Old relationships have to be left behind because the person is now making a commitment to an entirely different person. Many people believe that commitment means loss of freedom, when it means just the opposite. Once a person chooses a partner for life, he or she becomes free to at least be general friends with those of the opposite sex, just as naturally as with those of the same sex and just like before, but there have to be restrictions and limits. People know what the boundaries are, within themselves. For example, there must be no flirting with persons of the opposite sex after a person gets married. The flirtations, signals, and games that single people used in an effort to encourage or discourage another person have to be gone when there is no possibility of a close relationship with that person. Only friendship can abide, and even those should be kept at a bit of a distance.

Any friendship should not be stronger than what exists in the marriage between the two people. Possibilities for non-sexual friendships with those of the opposite sex can and do open up after a person gets married and they shouldn't all close up, but, certain of those relationships should really be ended. Often, they end on their own. For various reasons, people need other people in their lives, aside from their marriage partner, and so they maintain some relationships. They can put a marriage in a danger zone, though.

There can be a jealousy that festers, within the other person, even when there is trust. You never want a friendship to crowd out the positives present in a marriage. You have to be careful about jealousy, though. It can be unfounded. It can be present to an excess. If you crowd out a partner, certain of their needs will not be being met. Always make an effort to be on good terms with a partner. If you are an outside person, do not crowd out one of the persons in the relationship. Care about both people in the relationship, unless you just absolutely can't. You may need to just back away and stay away, for a while.

Outside friendships must be kept in balance and both individuals in the marriage should be all right with the other person's friends. No spouse should ever use an outside friendship that they have, against their spouse. That is so dangerous and can alienate the spouse to the point of no return. Both men and women have been guilty of doing this and it can cause a marriage to come to a very quick and irreparable end. Quickly go to a counselor for mediation if there are problems in these areas. Also, do not ever gang up on your spouse with a friend who stands in your favor. That can be unfair. The spouse will not like it.

If friendships begin to cut into the marital relationship, as sometimes happens, someone will always get hurt. For the most part, friendships should not take the place of the relationship that is present in a marriage. Both men and women are capable of letting this happen. Some just do not think ahead. Such a situation doesn't usually set well with the other person in the marriage. Men can become too friendly with other men and they can become too macho and too chauvinistic and this can squeeze out the woman and intimidate her. She will feel, all too much, like she is in the minority. Women become too friendly with other women, and the woman who is the outsider becomes the confidante, instead, when the husband should be the confidante.

Friends can become intrusions into a marriage, sometimes without really meaning to. I'm not indicating that outside people should be booted out of the lives of people who are in marriages, as sometimes unfortunately and prematurely happens, but I am indicating that partners in a marriage should sometimes put the brakes on, in their relationships with outside people and in what they allow themselves to be involved in. This would also include relationships with relatives. Married people need to set standards and rules—certainly for themselves. It may be that certain people who are affecting the lives of the couple should be seen less, or be more distanced (by words and/or attitude). This can be done respectfully, and with kindness.

With reference to fidelity, once you are married to that one special person, there is no room for sexual experimentation or relationships with other people. Some people choose to not have any sex before marriage and they do not believe in being unfaithful to their spouse, during the course of their marriage. When a person marries, he or she is choosing to have a faithful sexual relationship and to be set apart from the variety of the more superficial relationships that are available to people. With the right attitudes, a good sex life and binding intimacies can be strong and have depth. The two people should be each other's best friend. They should be in each other's corner. The two people will be building for the future and the future will continue to come as long as they're both alive.

In the beginning is romantic love, which people fall out of. The idealized romanticized love illusion is usually shattered. One falls out of this kind of love and one must work through the related period of disillusionment and transition as they move into a new conception of love, based not on projected needs but on a realistic appraisal of one another and based on a deep valuing of each other as being unique individuals. This is what the couple carries with them into old age, if they stay together that long. Too many people have to be alone during old age, because they were divorced or they never married. Marriage has its advantages and its positives; some of them relate to the later stages of marriage and life in general. It is good to grow old with a life partner. No one wants to be alone in their old age—not if they can avoid it.

Developing right attitudes is a primary ingredient for success in marriage, all the way through. Without right attitudes, everything can spin out of control. Every once in a while, both husband and wife need to check their attitude, and fine-tune it if it isn't quite right and if it is putting the marriage in a weakened and below-average zone. A spouse can sour towards the other spouse, and that can really be an attitude problem. It ties in with respect. Both spouses have to decide to respect the other, and to treat the other respectfully, and fairly. Without enough respect, much can come into conflict. It is not healthy to allow in sexism, for example. It can sneak in, at any bend or turn. Also, it is good to continually keep in mind what it is that you like about the other person. Don't let those revelations drop or get over-shadowed. There is also the area of role expectations. The way role expectations fall, in the domain of human sexuality, is in the way partners perceive their own masculinity or femininity. When there's an attitude change, and less respect, roles can shift and change and this can bring about chaos and turmoil.

Parents, relatives, and other adults in a young person's life behave differently towards each young person, from the very beginning (from birth on) and they, therefore, contribute to shaping children's personalities into becoming the typical masculine or feminine ones. For example, girls receive certain kinds of toys, and so do boys. Such toys begin programming or conditioning children from very early on. Also, boys are dressed differently than girls are and they often do different family chores than girls do. Generally, sex roles, and behaviors and mannerisms, are learned from a young age, and they become cumulative, and get ingrained. The essence of a person has come about by slow and gradual development. Children also learn a great deal when they observe other children, at the schools they attend.

Children raised around values where roles are sharply defined and where there is no crossing over of roles, tend to be more traditional in their marriage and with their childrearing, after they've had children. However, some marrieds depart from a traditional focus and they exercise occasional role reversals. Both venture over into the others' role arena, in other words. They trade, focus on, and take turns doing whatever tasks are at-hand, whether the particular task or tasks are traditionally considered to be feminine, or masculine. Some do this for expediency; some do this simply because they believe in it. Those who do this for expediency may still have basic traditional values and beliefs, about roles and about masculinity and femininity. But, they're practical people, too, and they realize that whatever needs to be done needs to be done by whoever happens to be traveling along the path of where the task or chore tends to be or is going to be.

Personal values and political choices can determine how a couple will run their household, too, just like expediency or necessity can. Communication about these issues should take place early on, before the two are even married, and communication about these subjects should be pointed and specific. On some issues, both should know how the other stands on key subjects before they are married. (Religion should be discussed, for sure.) The subject of sexism and having 50-50 input and value in the marriage should actually be discussed in a formal and definitive way. In marriage, how life is to be organized and lived should have at least general mutual agreement or the couple will not be very happy when certain difficulties roll in. They may not want to stay together because of friction. There will be too much arguing, for one thing. Belief in masculine and feminine roles should be discussed and generally, if not specifically, agreed upon. Political beliefs, especially in this day and age, are very important. Degree of happiness aligns with certain 'similarities'. The notion of 'friend or foe' will occasionally crop up. Many people are choosing to be an Independent, politically. Some do not consistently vote one party. You don't want to become adversarial in a relationship.

If you get into a marriage and find out that the other person in the marriage does not agree with you about essential matters, then there will be discord, unless someone changes (and they may never change). No one can count on someone changing or changing on time. Marriages often dissolve because of the 'too little too late' scenario. Of course, you don't want to expect too much, but when it becomes apparent that someone actually thinks very different than the other person thinks and has been regularly dragging their feet relative to co-operation, then it can really become 'too little too late'. The person does not want to change or co-operate, in other words. There are some who think they are right all the time and that they can do no wrong. They constantly argue and defend their position, whether they are right or wrong. They can be a real thorn in the flesh if you have to be around them. They are excessively defensive, and even obnoxious. They are self-strivers and they so often strive at wrong times. Get to know the person well before you decide to get married. Marriage is give and take.

Keep in mind that a 50-50 relationship will enable both people to view the other person as being fair-minded. Be very careful to avoid sexism. Sexism can be given a percentage in a marriage. it can be present any percent of the time. It can be smothering so that one person has no individuality. They cannot even be a person. Sexism is the same as chauvinism, wherever it is found. There can be male chauvinism, but there can also be female chauvinism, or sexism. In today's society, some women carry their independence (from men) a little too far and become too disrespectful and usurping when they are around men. Any rudeness or harsh and abrupt one-upping is unkind. It is usually out of order regardless of the gender and more people should try to be more diplomatic.

Several issues need to be discussed before the marriage takes place, and the subject of roles—whether to be traditional or non-traditional about them—is only one of those issues. Because political leanings are a related issue to roles, they should be discussed more in-depth than just surface. Religion is another one of these issues and it can sometimes relate to political inclinations and views about roles. Too many marrieds put sex first and think that if they are fine in the bedroom, they will be fine regarding everything else. Nothing could be further from the truth. As a result, the couple neglects to find essential things out about the other person until after the wedding. Then it can be too late, if differences are present and if each feels strongly about their own views.

Quite a few people in this world marry someone who is not right for them. Some couples stay celibate before they marry and there is more emphasis on finding other things out about the other person, early-on. They focus more on getting to know the other person. There is a time that gets set aside for actual courting. The emphasis is on 'getting to know you', rather than on sex and gratification. You don't enter a relationship to have fun. Fun should be very background. You enter a relationship to get to know the other person. When there are enough commonalities, each person can, then, grow to care about the other person and establish a binding relationship of a permanent type.

Some single people, however, are not interested in that kind of courtship, and sex is a part of their life and they do not wish to be celibate or to save themselves for marriage. To each his or her own. Let people live how they want and be what they want, because they're going to do that and be that way, anyway. In truth, though, not everyone should live how they want to live and be the way they want to be, if it is hurting themselves, others, or society. Some people live in atrocious immorality and it is hurting others and the world. It's hurting the very people who are inclined to be this way, though they may not be able to see that and may not wish to see that. Some people deserve chastisements and rebukes but even then, they'll stay stubborn and continue doing what they're doing. They'll constantly venture into doing new, similar things. Being involved in illegal pornography, in any way, is a good example of this.

Quite a few people like to watch pornography, or see it in print. There can be no proper courtship, for marriage, if one or both in a couple are watching pornography. All the right aspects of courtship will be blocked. Everything goes in the wrong direction. Being affected by pornography in adverse ways has been a problem for society for a long time. It can be important to find out how someone feels about pornography before getting involved with that person. What are the person's values, in general, too—look into that. Become a detective, of sorts, or think of yourself as an investigative reporter (who reports to yourself). Do not commit to someone who you really don't know. Stay aloof until you do, even if you think you might lose that person. You only really get to know a person by spending enough quality time with that person. It can be hard to find good places to go and good things to do, these days, and everything costs money, but formal dating can still take place.

Both men and women should go into relationships, as detectives. Realize, however, that no one is perfect. Some things you just have to let slide…but not the real important things. Look for red flags and warning signals. These days, you pretty much have to. Be yourself. Make sure the other person is being him or herself, too. People learn to be actors. They learn to play games. If there are too many negatives, get out and move on, fast, so you'll have time to find someone much less iffy, or not iffy, at all. Set, as a goal, finding the best marriage partner you can as fast as you can, before you get too old. Work hard at the relationship if you find it.

# *Chapter 5*

## Sex-related Issues

Sex in marriage can be successful or unsuccessful; it can cause a marriage to work or not work, for the two individuals. If there are sexual dysfunctions, either psychological or physiological-based, sex therapy is a growing business that should not be ruled out because of embarrassment that might be present or because of fear that therapy cannot help. Also, many physicians are trained to detect physiological problems in the male or female, if the problem or problems are physiological. Sometimes people delay going to professionals for too long a period of time, and their marriage disintegrates in the meantime. A good rule of thumb is: seek out as many of the best resources as possible, be they people, books or DVD's, or information found on the computer or smartphone, and get help for your problems immediately and all along the way if they are present and if they persist. Don't be a puppet or a stone all your life. Take charge. Do something about your marital problems.

Unfortunately, many young couples wait too long, thinking the sexual problems in their marriage will go away by themselves or miraculously get fixed, when oftentimes, things end out getting worse. Impotency is a problem in some marriages. Many men experience impotency at different times, or even all the time. Usually, this is psychological and it can relate to inexperience, stress, fear, and inadequate feelings about masculinity. It can also relate to fatigue. Sometimes, however, impotency is physiological. Today, there are products that can be purchased and used to increase sexual potency and ability. A doctor should first be consulted, however. With good counseling and direction, sexual problems can be overcome.

Another problem in a marriage can be female frigidity. It, too, can be overcome. There are new products that can stimulate sexual interest and these products are not pornographic, they're medical. There are material devices that can be used. Each person needs to learn about the other's sexual needs and behaviors, and to learn to adapt to the other person, in that respect. Life is too short to allow sexual problems to reduce one's quality of life. Never forget communication, either; partners must talk things through. Whether two people feel like it or not, sitting down and talking things over can clear up misunderstandings and help to solve problems.

If there are sexual problems in a marriage, usually there is a need for psychological counseling because, oftentimes, sexual failure causes certain feelings to take root inside of both partner's minds, and some of these feelings can be negative and damaging. Even if the problem has been, or is a physiological or a medical one, the psychological aspect still needs to be addressed. For example, lack of expectation can cause frustration so that lack of effort can become routine. Lack of effort can mean no sex, whatsoever. If a positive change is to occur, then there has to be renewed effort, and reconditioning may be needed. There may have to be a psychological reprogramming. Something medical might be needed. Something medical could be wrong. Keep it all simple, though. Problems are meant to be solved.

Many people believe that the liberated woman concept emasculates males and causes impotency to increase. Hence, there has been a flourishing of impotency or erectile dysfunction products on the market. That liberated women emasculate men is probably true—at least in part and at least some of the time—but it shouldn't have to be a cause of impotency. It's way off-center if men let it be a cause. It is a 'choice' to let it be a cause, or to not. It all relates to attitude, and to confidence. Often, men should be happy for women who are getting things done and getting ahead. They should be happy for women when women are happy. They should be happy for women when women are confident and upbeat. Women deserve to have rights in this world, the same as men do. It's well past the time when women should be able to exercise their rights.

Unfortunately, even though women have been given certain rights, by law, they are often not given these rights behind the scenes and behind closed doors. It's been a man's world for such a long period of time and that is why changes for women have been going slow, particularly in some societies around the world. Men are the ones who go into combat when fighting wars. They tend to be the head of the household. They have higher business positions, as a whole. They run businesses, and governments. Frankly, true and thorough or complete change may never completely come for women. Women work very hard, though, and for this reason they deserve equal status in both the home and the workplace. Many times, women work harder than men do. Women are, on average, quite fastidious, especially with regards to physical work. Women are very good with their hands and their fingers. Often, women work too hard and do not get enough support. When women get home after a hard-day's work, they can be too tired and too unfocused to think much about having sex. Their mind can be on work, and this, of course, happens to men, too. Marriages can suffer, because of evening fatigue.

The truth is, men should have their own confidence, independent of women, and vice versa. A man should have a confidence in himself that is equal to the confidence that a woman has in herself, since both men and women are separate individuals and since both men and women are needed and need to live and survive on this planet. Women should be making the same kind of money that men make for the same kind of labor and they don't, usually. Many women inherit money, though. Men usually die several years before their wife does. Workplace promotions should be based on merit and even seniority and they shouldn't be based on gender. Suze Orman has been a voice on finances for these kinds of truths but she is just one of the few women entrepreneurs that are out there speaking for women. She's been inspirational, and her practical ideas have been helpful to both men and women but perhaps, more so, to women.

Both men and women have to work, especially these days. Men used to be the working backbone of this country, but our culture has changed. With regards to working, fair is fair. Receiving equal pay for equal work, regardless of sex difference, is what is fair. Also, no sexual harassment is allowed at the workplace in America any more and this is a good thing. Some women were forced to quit a job because of badly-behaved men. Some women were not promoted or given raises if they refused a higher-up man's advances. These disgusting days are now gone, for the most part. Men or now afraid to harass women in any way, at the workplace. Women stand together, and get these men fired or put behind bars. It's all part of the Me Too Movement. Since the beginning of the 21st Century, more women have gradually been put in higher positions. Women are starting their own companies, too, and they are succeeding at business endeavors. The doors have been opening more and more for women and the sky's the limit for those who push themselves. Fortunately, everyone has the right to earn a living any way they can, as long as it's legal.

You're seeing way more women in action movies, too. Many of these action-film women end out fighting men. They fight them with their bodies and with weapons. They know Judo and Karate, et al. These action-film women are also very smart. Their ability to fight can almost seem miraculous. Such films help to give more status to women. One film especially comes to mind—*Columbiana* (2011) and Zoe Saldana was the lead character who ends out wiping out some corrupt, evil men. This film was a milestone movie for women because she seemed to be a real-life Wonder Woman. These films do not fall under the domain of your standard Chick Flicks. They not only make women look good, but they also cause some women to be feared (perhaps on a more subliminal level, and by men).

If men cannot share with women, in diverse ways, then they are not humanitarian. Women have value. They are very much needed in this world and they contribute a great deal to it. Some countries stunt and stifle women's potential. (And it isn't just certain Muslim factions and countries that treat women badly, either). In several countries, men call all the shots and women are actually persecuted, oppressed, derided, and ridiculed. (Some of them are put to death and killed, mainly in Muslim countries). Many men take advantage of women and thwart their advancing. Women are not as strong as men are, physically, and so men take advantage of that physical weakness. (Women can be much faster than men, though, when it comes to certain kinds of work, but they generally do not have as much muscle power and physical strength, nor do they have as deep-sounding voices, which can sometimes be important for men to have.)

Some countries around the world have uncharitable and unmerciful dominant religions or they are godless; many freedoms in certain countries are stifled, including freedom of religion. You can forget about seeing Women's Rights and freedom of religion in some countries. Neither exists. We can only hope that they may exist in time, but freedom of religion won't ever exist in some countries. Women have more rights in the democratic countries and in the Free World.

In America, women fought for rights and have been able to prevail, in part because Christianity is present and it is a religion based on love and mercy, but also on hard work. Women's Rights is not, necessarily, the same as Feminism. Feminism tends to, politically, be more to the Left and it includes some issues that were not fought by way of the Women's Rights movement. People do not separate the two in their mind. Feminism includes for all of the Women's Rights issues but Women's Rights only includes for some of the Feminism issues. The Muslims would do well to separate the two (and give women more rights). In certain countries, where there is no mercy, women have been imprisoned, tortured, and/or killed, for fighting for Women's Rights. Men will say "well if you give women an inch, they'll take a mile" but some women should have had that mile a long time ago. Some rights are good. Some may not be as good. But, some factions try to withhold all rights for women.

It would be more than interesting if sex studies were to ever get done that are not padded, stacked, and twisted and that relate to Muslim countries, especially relative to the women's honest thoughts and attitudes about sex, and about gender and roles, and to find out what those results were. Some Muslim men have more than one wife; some even have several wives. Some Muslim girls come in as teenage, or even as child brides. Some of these young girls are married off to men who are old. Many wives are beaten. Older men, even very old men, end out having sex with girls that could be the age of their daughters and even granddaughters. Some women are forced to have sex against their will. Marriages should always be about two-way consenting and any consenting should not be coerced. Frankly, some Muslim marriages are oppressive—mainly for the women. Husbands have been known to rape a wife or they'll coerce their wife into having sex when it is against her will. Sometimes, when sex is forced on them and sex is not wanted, they are even forced or coerced into acting like they liked it. It is only this way with some Muslim men, though, and so many Muslim women are not happy in their marriage but what can they do? They grab hold of what they can that gives them security and happiness but happiness is relative and not often around for them. Their happiness is but partial. True, happiness amount can shift from time to time, but it is always relative. Many Muslim men have not considered the happiness of Muslim women, enough or at all.

A happiness scale from one to ten is a good way to ascertain one's happiness but when a happiness amount is ascertained, to what degree is the individual comparing their happiness with that of others, and should they be doing that? I say, yes, to a point an individual can do that as long as it is in the realm of comparison and is relating to similar people and circumstances. It is good to be realistic. A person can boost their happiness level by changing some things in their life but happiness is also attitudinal. For sure, happiness is situational and some people are unable to change too much about their life. More women are happy in the United States than they are in other countries because the USA has bounty and is a prosperous country.

Again, Feminism is not the same as the Women's Rights, via the Women's Rights Movement. Women's Rights related to voting, initially, then they moved to working and jobs, then they moved to pay amount, benefits, and somewhat to jobs. Only some would include the pill and abortion in with Women's Rights. Some would include gay rights relative to women, as well. A number of people wouldn't, though, and would affirm that Women's Rights only have to do with jobs and work. The key crux of the Women's Movement is equal rights and equality. It is with Feminism, too, but Feminism is different, having different applications.

Usually sex is kept out of the workplace. It is supposed to be. Work is not a place for recreation. Concentration and focus at work is not supposed to be on sex. Ideally, when two people get married and love each other, sex will always stay in their own bedroom. Committed marrieds will not have wandering eyes. They'll keep an emotional distance from anyone who is attractive at the workplace.

It's up to each individual to develop a confidence level high enough to allow themselves to function competently in all areas of life, including in the bedroom. It takes work, and it takes thinking things through and not giving up in defeat. It will require intelligent thought to establish and keep a good sex life. If there are problems, each individual will have to develop their own sound mind, by their own efforts or by taking time out to seek outside help, if that is what's necessary. Outside help can bring quicker results, generally, compared with if a person just tries to bumble through everything on their own. Each person should be concerned about their own development, and about the quality of their development. Some people do not want to seek outside help, because of arrogance, usually, or because of fear, but it is really a feather in one's cap if they seek outside help because doing so reveals that they are smart people who realize that their own growth and development is their responsibility and that they are on this Earth to improve as human beings. Self-improvement is a race to be run, actually. Self-improvement is always brought into a marriage.

Harboring guilt is not good for a marriage. Sometimes guilt can manifest itself as under-confidence. If a person has led an immoral life or partaken in sexual immorality, pornography, or even in some kind or kinds of sexual deviancy, it may be that dysfunctions in a marriage will be caused by this past, although, some very immoral people have had uncomplicated and generally well-functioning sex lives so this is not an ironclad outcome or by-product of that kind of behavior. Conscience has a lot to do with outlook, though, and with how one sees him or herself. Also, conscience affects behavior, both consciously and unconsciously. Conscience can affect behavior and behavior can affect a marriage.

There may be times when one person will want to give up. They'll get too discouraged. This person can be single or partnered in some way. Life in general can appear hopeless to anyone at any time. What they want and even need can seem hopeless. They are not able to attain what they want or need. They may or may not have a reasonable assessment of their own abilities or of what is going on around them. Sad people have been increasing in number and for a number of reasons. Some reasons are totally legitimate. Some are uncontrollable. Many reasons are external and some are because of a morally-declining society. Much, too, has to do with personal finances and the economy. It may appear to some that society is not declining but overall, it is, and has been since about 1995. Just because some moral virtues and strength are being seen here and there doesn't mean that there isn't an overall decline going on.

Because so many people are sad or sadder these days, this means that people need to start being nicer to other people, and start lifting more people up. This will help to reduce the sadness. To say to someone "don't give up" and "don't get discouraged" is often not enough. These are surface statements and usually someone who has lost hope and is discouraged needs to hear much more than to just hear surface statements. They need good professional help, before they get any sadder. They might need to get around some new people, some of the time. The sadness they are feeling could relate to some of the people, presently, in their life. People can become sad within a marriage, too. A number of people, these days, are not happy in their overall family. Quite a few people are not that happy and they keep their feelings to themselves. Happiness is relative, and it ebbs and flows.

When there are problems that cause pain, unhappiness, and frustration in a couple's sex life, every factor needs to be considered so the problems can begin to be solved. Sex therapy is an area or practice that many professionals do not feel comfortable working in; however, it is an area that is opening up for trained professionals. Some non-professional people have been getting into this and have been pulling clients over to themselves. They lack education and training, and don't have the foundation of a related college or university degree. Sex therapy is an area for the psychiatrist, the psychologist, or the trained and formally-educated counselor. Some of these professionals specialize in sex therapy. As noted earlier, a few sex therapists have such related academic degrees, but many sex therapists do not. Some of them might be good and may have gone through some kind of training program, somewhere.

Sex therapy is really not an area for the novice, the uneducated, or the fly-by-night. Sex therapists must take into account the whole person, and every component of a person—both as an individual, and as a person functioning within a marriage and in combination with a mate. The spiritual ties in too, when there is treatment of the whole person, and many trained professionals usually try to include the spiritual when they are helping patients or clients. Some don't, but that doesn't mean they aren't good. Actually, some clients aren't seeking the spiritual anyway, only the psychological. Some professionals are extremely good as sex therapists; others just don't have the knack but they may still be good counselors. It may not hurt, at times, to have two counselors.

If sex is bad in a marriage, there is apt to be arguing and fighting, or, a quiet resignation. There can be a sexual dysfunction. A frustration and an unhappiness will linger. Loss of respect for the dysfunctional partner, and self-pity, can drive the two people apart. All this can cause over-reactions to trivial things that are affecting the marriage. Negative emotions can take over. One or both can become harsh and overly reactive. The sooner the couple can get into counseling and therapy, with a good professional or professionals, the better it will be for both of them. Infidelity can enter into such struggling marriages. A marriage can get off-balance. Sadly, alcoholism, drug abuse, gambling, or excessive working can come on the scene, as ways to supplant frustration and unhappiness. This, of course, just brings on more problems. Sex problems can be serious, and because of them, other problems can come on the scene that are equally, if not more taxing. Other problems can cloak the sex problems, too. This is why professional help is needed.

Let's assume there is healthy sexuality and good sex in a marriage. What basics exist in such a marriage to make the sex life good? Probably the most unifying basic is that of communication. If a couple is good at verbal communication, and communicate a great deal with each other, they are apt to be good at their two-way sexual communication, too. This means that before and during sex they will give each other cues about sexual direction and they will let the partner know what gives them pleasure or what is giving them pleasure at a given time (or what does not give them pleasure or what is not giving them pleasure at a given time). Each partner is sensitive and receptive to the cues and sexual directives that the other partner is giving. This freedom in their overall communicating can enable the couple to allow more variety into their sex life (if that is what they want) because this sensitivity and receptivity allows them to experiment and to try new ways of sexual expression for greater sexual fulfillment.

Some couples will sometimes drink alcohol before having sex. Alcohol may cause some inhibitions to subside but it may also deaden or decrease physical feeling and sensation. The most sexually-successful couples do not feel that they need alcohol to help them with their sex life. If they drink some alcohol on occasion, it's not because they need it to help their sex life. Alcohol, in general, might be of some help, briefly and at times, but it's of less help than many people believe.

Many young people use alcohol. Many a young lady has been seduced because of alcohol, in large part because of drinking too much. Some will drink the same amount as the man drinks but because they are smaller and weigh less, they get intoxicated faster, which is what some young men are hoping will happen, for obvious reasons. To add to this, women have less water in their body so the alcohol does not get as well diluted. They also tend to have more fat in their body and fat does not absorb alcohol so more alcohol ends out going in their blood. Women produce less of the enzyme that contributes to processing alcohol, too, so all in all, men have it over a barrel when it comes to being able to hold their liquor better than women do. Men will be more in control than the girl or woman is, in other words, and, they will have more pleasure, sexually, than the woman will because she might be blitzed. Such a strategy is heightened selfishness. Some men have plied women with alcohol for this very reason, but for more sensible people, little to no alcohol is needed for good sexual relationships.

Caring for the other person is, of course, a prerequisite for having a good, consistent sex life. Self-seeking and self-indulgent sex will only cause frustration and unhappiness for both people. Sex is something partners do for each other and not just with each other. For people who care about each other, every time they have sex they will be able to express their caring, and express the love they have for each other, as well. This is the ideal and the ideal can be present if the two people will it to be.

Usually, if two people care about each other they will also care about any children they have. By intercourse and procreation, through pregnancy and delivery, when a baby is born, the couple will experience a tremendous sense of achievement and accomplishment. Having a baby can become a major milestone in their lives. It can add to their own individual feelings of masculinity and femininity and to their sense that their union has been important. The baby can bring the two together, too, assuming they are prepared to have the baby. The baby can unite the couple, in special and diverse ways. In a way, the baby will be half his and half hers, but a better way to look at it is that the baby a part of both of them. The baby links the couple in a new and unique way. Sex should be in a marriage to produce pleasure, but also to produce children. Biologically, human beings are made to experience both.

Again, a marriage requires good communication, as fuel for the marriage. Communicating helps the couple to get through each day and to complete necessary daily tasks. Assuming they are able to successfully talk about things, as they happen and as they come up, the potential to get more done will be there. With good verbal communication, there are two major areas that are of concern. The first simply relates to going about expressing true feelings all along the way. The second relates to conflict and confrontation, otherwise known as fighting.

Some couples may need help in the area of confrontation and conflict. They may need a third party to be present, while they are arguing. If you think this is easy work for a professional, you're wrong. Being a type of referee can be rough counseling. (Just watch a show like *Dr. Phil* and you will see how hard it can be.) It's a rough experience for the couple. It can be adversarial. It often is. A feuding couple needs a setting where they can air their differences with a trained third party who is there to guide them through it. Good results can come from this, but the results can also be negative. Some couples need to acquire actual communication skills. One person might be rude, overbearing, and sarcastic. Both people could be, when it comes right down to it. After any kind of open feuding or arguing takes place, a couple will need time out. They may need even as long as a week so they can sort everything out properly.

Couples should not be afraid to have what I refer to as productive spats. These spats (versus really heated arguments) should not go past a certain point relative to overt anger. Anger has to be kept down as the couple converses and discusses and they will have to stop themselves from raising their voice. Arguing couples can disagree if they must, since each one is their own person, but they should meet somewhere in the middle when they can. Whatever is at-issue, they have to communicate all important details. There should be back and forth talk and then more back and forth talk until everything necessary has been put into the discussion (or the argument). It is better to keep disagreements at the discussion level whenever possible. A couple may need to have a second discussion about what is at-issue.

One person of the two may have to move over for the other person, a little or a lot, temporarily or permanently, but situations can change after a time so the pendulum can always swing back to the other person's view or favor. Still and all, it does not seem quite right when one person always gets their way and wins the argument. Logically, lopsided prevailing does not seem right. It's not law of averages. In any event, for the efforts expended, all arguments have to be productive—or what's the point of having a confrontation. Something must be gained from the arguing. What sometimes happens is that one will walk away in a huff so nothing gets resolved. This is why both should stay level and be even-keeled as they are talking. Talk through the conflict, not part-way through it.

Sometimes couples are on the same wavelength when it comes to communicating, in general. Such couples are very fortunate because so often, couples don't think alike so they don't converse all that smoothly. Some couples argue a great deal and pretty soon it all begins to wear too thin. Obviously, some couples very definitely need an intermediary, as a counselor, psychologist, or even a minister. A best friend of one party does not usually work. It can add to the discord. The other person might feel ganged up on.

When it comes to being rude, it is often how something is said, versus what is being said. There are times when what accent is put on what words matters. In other words, the whole meaning can be changed if the accent is put on another word or syllable, relative to what is said. But, at times, it isn't even that—it's just the particular way that something is said. In relationships, these kinds of things matter. A partner will pick up on how something is said. If a partner is always using tricks and deceptions and maneuvers when they are fighting, the other partner will become grievously upset. They'll certainly pick up on that. Play everything straight and fair. Be thorough and direct and absolutely, do not play games. Be extremely careful about hitting below the belt, too. Hitting below the belt is unfair fighting.

I've written three poems about rudeness. Some other of my poems make note of it. I've written up to 470 poems and short works and the majority of them would be of help to married couples (since marriage and general counseling is my field). Education has also been my field and the majority of the poems and short works are generally or specifically educational and education helps everybody. The title of my three more-specific 'rude' poems are *Rudeness*, *Rudosity*, and *Rude People*. Some of my other poems relate to rudeness, too. In a marriage, or any relationship, being rude can be quite damaging. It also causes unhappiness. Rudeness is the same as slighting and even intimidating and so, really, how is that good? You're striving for co-operation, unification, respect, and happiness in a marriage. Rudeness can be manipulation and an effort to coerce. It breeds alienation and resentment so how does that help any relationship?

Also, when it comes to complaining, be careful about when and how you do it. When you openly <u>complain</u>, you then feel you must stay in that mode if nothing changes. You will be <u>grumbling</u>, as a result. Sometimes it's best to keep your complaints secret, depending on the situation. It's like when you give an ultimatum. You always have to follow through with it. If you do complain, choose a good time to do it and frame your complaint in a thoughtful and intelligent way.

Communication skills need to be consciously learned, and then consciously applied on a continual basis, whether people are married or are single. People need to learn how to get their points across, to express their ideas and wishes articulately and intelligently, and to handle confrontation and conflict. In a marriage, if one or both persons lack these skills, they need an arbitrator or facilitator who is trained as a therapist and who has an education that relates to psychiatry, psychology, or counseling. They need someone who's objective and who won't take sides. Without good communication, sex in the marriage will wane and not mean as much to the two people.

There are three keys to a good marriage. If they are applied, there will be more closeness, in general (including in the bedroom). First, the couple should be practical about everything that a couple thinks and does. Second, the couple should never play mind games with each other and engage in trickery and manipulation. Third, each partner should continually be working and doing something, only resting when absolutely necessary. Being lazy and having little initiative will cause resentment and will harm a marriage, and any relationship, for that matter.

# Chapter 6

# Overcoming Problems

We all live in a world with more than surface-level concerns, and sometimes people's lives get very complicated and too much can happen too fast. If people don't handle matters effectively, as things are affecting their life and when things are affecting their life, problems will stay around so that when new things happen that affect them and that also need the people's time and attention, their problems will mount and can even multiply and compound if there are enough incoming problems because the people will still have all those previous problems that they hadn't resolved earlier. They'll just have too many problems. They can then get way too overloaded, all because they did not deal with their first problems when they first hit. Therefore, people need to have and to develop communication skills and use them early on and all along the way. Otherwise, they won't be able to work through their problems very quickly, or quickly enough. They also won't be able to work through their problems very well. It will essentially all be dead end. All that can be done when stacked-up problems are around is to leave certain ones be, and that never works.

You want to get as much behind you as you can. True, some problems will always be around. You can't do much about certain problems. Some problems won't go away. You may need an attitude change or to see something differently. But, it is the problems that can be fixed and resolved that need to be fixed and resolved. It's not good to get lax and lazy about such issues, and to procrastinate when problems need immediate attention. Seeing a counselor or other professional can help to put the focus on key problems, and help to get them resolved. Any counseling has to be purposeful.

Some problems can be worked through with a counselor, but some have to be worked out by the couple. A counselor can't do everything. In fact, sometimes counselors will bounce it all back into the couple's court, anyway. A couple should never assume that a counselor can solve their problems and so, the couple will have to brush up on communication skills, no matter what. Counselors may only guide people along so they can find their own resolutions. Counselors may not always be the 'be all end all' because there could be other problems, too—some very serious ones—and the counselor might not even know about those things yet. Only certain problems come up during a counseling session, and you cannot rush things.

Keep in mind—and this is very important—that many men do not talk as much as women do. So, they cannot get their points across as often as women do and they cannot generally defend themselves in the same way that women can. Men say less, but what they say has importance, usually, but not in every case, especially if they get cut off. Women need to respect the fact that men do not talk as much as they talk, on average. Too many women take advantages of men's reserve or of their talking less and they become too bossy and domineering. They fill in the gap of the lack of talking and will talk more than the man. Sometimes, they don't mean to take advantage of the situation. Other times, they aren't really thinking about it, one way or the other.

When there is no 50-50 relationship, you often find sexism. Sexism can be intentional, or inadvertent and accidental. Such relationships will need work, and probably some counseling. If there is love, no one should mind positive shifts and tweaks in their relationship. Two people should be open to whatever is positive and best. If one person want the other person in the relationship to be 'over them', then that should be accepted, too, because some religions teach this. However, this can be carried way too far. Some religions are now changing, some, as to how they view male headship, and they have given women better place and more respect. Some are now giving women full equality with men. Others are holding back. Views of different Faiths are based on their own teachings.

Some women need to give the man more space, and value what the man says a lot more often than they do. Some women need to get real and accept this and put listening more into practice. Women have been known to interrupt too often so they have to try to avoid doing that. Men have rights, too, in other words. Some women seem to forget this. Men know more than some women might think; they're quick to assess and size up matters. They can especially see the large picture and zero in on what's important. Many men tend to have this knack. There are gender differences—or inclinations is a better word—but this does not mean that one sex is superior and more important than the other. Both sexes are equally important and contribute to the relationship in helpful and useful ways. Both people in a relationship have equal personage.

Another point to be made about men, in their favor, is that they're the ones who have had to do the actual fighting, in wars. They've also been almost all of the principle builders. Most do not think about it but men have been almost all of the principle inventors, over a period of time. They've invented practically everything, including airplanes, guns, bombs, ships, and machine parts. They have not been the stay-at-home gender, like women have been. Keep in mind that men aren't nurturers. They don't nurture, coddle, or comfort, to the extent that women do. They encourage, and give out strength, but they are not the nurturers. There are sex differences and trait differences and if you try to get men to go against their natural inclinations, to be real, most of them won't be happy about that and they'll let you know it.

Deep down, most men who are in the mainstream do not have genuine respect for men who act and/or are feminine and for women who act and/or are masculine. They may like them as people, but not really respect them. This has been changing but most people prefer to see conformity to society norms and to what seems most usual. (There are still norms in society even though society seems to have changed as much as it has.) Just because a man may look feminine and have feminine tendencies doesn't mean that he has to incline himself that way. He can act like a man and try to look like a man. It's the same with women who may look masculine and have masculine qualities. In as much as they are able to do, all people could strive to look and be in conformity with their natural gender. Many a questioning and confused person has done this and life turned out all-right for them. It's all in the attitude and in the resolve. If someone wants to do something bad enough, they will, and it's as simple as that. They'll stick to it, too. The same applies if they choose to go the other way, too. Some people are not happy in their own skin, and they want to change direction. It is always all about choices.

It can be very hard for some people to continue living in a way that was expected of them, by others, if they find that path to be too difficult. It is wrong to treat these people badly. If some people who were living in certain countries to change gender or be into same-sex relationships, they would be killed. Some would be tortured, first. No one is made to compromise their own beliefs in contemporary democracies but parts of society may shun those who go against the principal ways and views that run that society. Regardless of what anyone's beliefs are on any subject or in any area, that person should periodically review their beliefs. Beliefs sometimes change and are modified. This happens to many people. Even some religious beliefs can be changed or modified but certain ones will probably always stay around if they are core beliefs and assuming a person has always been religious. Some religious teachings cannot change because no one is going to throw away the books they are based on, not in a free society.

Marriage is filled with challenges. Sometimes compromise holds a couple back because it may not be the best solution to a problem. This gets into the arena of submission and headship in a home. With submission and headship, one person has the final say about matters, and, the other person must allow that person to have the final say. This is one approach to order in a home. There should be agreement to this outlook, should a couple decide that this is their preference for how they want their marriage to be and their home to be run. Otherwise, the two people should decide on equal say for equal decisions and on equal decision-making all the way down the line. This is another approach to order in a home. However, this second approach can result in conflict because sometimes both will want their own decision to prevail over the other person's decision and both may hold firm to their position. This can cause long-term friction. It can result in lack of resolution. Chaos and disintegration can occur. A give-and-take approach is usually going to be better.

No one likes to think that someone else is smarter and more capable than they are about making decisions, especially when the decisions affect their own life; however, in a marriage where two are joined together and are functioning as a unit, it really shouldn't matter how the decisions are made as long as they are made and no one person becomes too unhappy. Some women don't give men enough of a chance to think through things and to make decisions, and that certainly isn't right. They refuse to give the man enough space. Some women act too fast and don't wait to discuss some matters with their husband. Some women are hyper and impulsive. Some men can be, too. Both men and women can be overbearing, and unfair, but if you are married, you must work together and make an effort to be in harmony. You must try to find the best solutions to your problems. Sometimes, you will have to step back and give the other person the space and final say.

Both men and women can have cyclical depression. They may go up and down/ high and low, somewhat, but the thread of depression goes through their day-to-day life all the time. Even when they experience an up or a high, they inwardly know that they are a depressed person. The depression often relates to unresolved conflicts and issues. However, depression is relative to all people. Depression has a range. Despair so often ties in with depression. So does disappointment so there is a 3-D there. Disappointment, depression, and despair can be a triangle of emotion.

Some people are minimally depressed and they are usually all-right, over all. It's the people who go beyond being minimally depressed who need the help. All need preventative help but it may not be there when it needs to be. Some need remedy help. That may not be there, either. Remedy help can be preventative help, some of the time. What is at root needs to be dug up so there is a clear consciousness of what has been causing the depression. Treatment should follow such an uprooting, but, there could be more than one cause, so <u>all</u> the causes have to be uprooted, and made clear. This is where counseling can come in.

If, in a marriage, the two people decide that the man will be the head of the home, then the wife has to be willing to allow for some occasional error. No marriage of this type should have a wife who is not strong and who is not able to express her thoughts and views. Women should be allowed to have their say. Frankly, a woman often knows more about a situation than the man does so when the man decides something it is often because of the woman's input. In an equal-say and equal-decide marriage, with 'enough' communication on whatever are the subjects of immediate concern, often a resolution or solution will come to light—and it will be something that both the husband and the wife will see and accept. It may not be seen immediately, but eventually it will be seen. This is where faith enters in. Some marriages are faith-based, but not all are.

In husband-as-head-of-the-home marriages, some husbands can become selfish, arrogant, abusive, and oppressive. They can stifle, hurt, and embarrass the wife because they are not loving and are too ego-absorbed. Even when there is just some of this, the women have to allow for occasional error because, like women, men are inclined to learn as they go, but if the man is an oppressive, self-inclined chauvinist (a sexist) and not very wise, the woman won't want to be able to accept his views. Lack of love, impulsiveness, poor judgment, and stubbornness will lead to problems and some can be devastating. Some men can be bullies and tyrants. No one likes being around them. Too much alcohol and/or too many drugs can adversely affect a man's judgment. It causes a wasting of time, for one thing, so important things don't get done. Also, some men are still immature and haven't yet grown up. They need time before they can get it all together. Still, if they are insensitive, oppressive, and arrogant, that doesn't life easy for anyone. Stubbornness can be very bad. When someone should change but they refuse to because of male ego, they are sometimes being chauvinists or sexist, assuming they are treating women badly, which they likely are.

On one level, if two become one and are as one, they will be alike and think alike and be concerned about the other, equally and as themselves, and they will want their partner to be happy, just like they want to be happy. Marriages should be 'Golden Rule'. Therefore, both people in a marriage should, at times, be willing to acquiesce to the other when it is clear and evident that they should. You need patience in a marriage. If a partner is seen as being equal, they will be treated equally. Love your partner as yourself is a good creed to adopt. Again, relationships are give and take.

It should be a natural thing to acquiesce if you love the person. True, marriage is also give and take, take and give. But, each spouse has to be ever ready to acquiesce, at least at times. Acquiescence has to be done by both, though, and at different times, obviously. (When there is a compromise, there is only partial-acquiescence.) Of course, both persons should demonstrate that they are capable of handling a home and a group of problems first, or no one is going to want to give the other person much space.

If you don't have trust in a person, don't marry the person. This is why it is important to get to know the person well before you marry them and the knot gets tied. Never marry a person you have too many doubts and reservations about; it's not wise; you would be gambling. Communication can help to bring about changes in both people, remember, but if proper and needed change is not seen in the other person relative to key matters, patience will wane or be lost. Keep in mind that a husband and wife will chisel and shape and mold each other, they're both a little like potters or sculptors. This is supposed to be happening, as both undergo constructive change. It should not be viewed as being negative.

If a man is tyrannical (and some men are) then the woman isn't going to want to give the man very much space and who can blame her? She won't want her children exposed to tyrannical judgment and behavior, either. She will defend and fight for her own position, believing it to be the more sound and reasonable. She will believe that her position has the greatest positive affect on the greatest number of people, which includes herself. Some women are far from perfect, though. Anyone can have premature judgments about issues. It's always good to wait until all the information is in. It's always good to see if a second look at everything works. There are times when a woman can be wrong in her assessment and outlook. Women can be selfish and self-centered, just like men can be. Sometimes, certain women at certain times need to put on the brakes, and shine a light on what is happening and take time out to consider the other person's views.

If a woman is hyper, inconsistent, empty-headed, self-absorbed, and uses poor judgment, then the man isn't going to want to give the woman very much space. Marry someone you respect, or you can run into these kinds of problems. Young marrieds will have some of their undeveloped negative qualities coming through, some of the time and because they are growing, but if there is too much of what is negative and too much selfishness and it seems to linger, there will be problems. It considerably helps to have some genuine respect for the other person. Things generally get handled more peacefully. Communication will be better.

If two people get to know each other well before they are married, they can spot-check for negative and selfish behaviors. This is why it is important to go slow when first meeting a person of the opposite sex. Sadly, too many people jump into bed and their judgment gets clouded. Of course they're going to try to please the other and get along, at first, because they want the relationship to get launched. Once it gets launched, out comes the real person. The word, courtship, may be an old-fashioned one but it remains an important word because it implies that two people should take their time to get to really know each other before they allow themselves to permanently bond. One woman I counseled got her hopes up and thought she had found 'the one' and she impulsively jumped in too fast only to find out that the man had done time for pushing drugs. She also found out that he was a chauvinist to the core...because of some of the behaviors she gradually observed. Another woman found out that the man she fell in love with was still married. This, of course, is very common, though who can compile exact statistics. Many will keep that scenario secret.

One only needs to watch relationship shows like the ones that have been hosted by Phil Donahue, Sally Jesse Raphael, Oprah Winfrey, Montel Williams, Jerry Springer, Maury Povitch, Arsenio Hall, Dr. Phil, Steve Wilkos, Bill Cunningham, Robert Irvine, and Steve Harvey to become aware of lies that have been told and deceptions that have taken place in relationships. Most of these talk-show people have not been trained counselors or psychologists. Still, they are terrific at what they do and what they have done has been tough stuff. All the fisticuffs can be a bit much on some of these shows. Counselors and psychologists don't have security men in the room with them. They want to avoid fisticuffs.

Try to stay away from deception, in any relationship. 'Oh what a tangled web we weave when first we practice to deceive'. Try very hard to never, ever lie. There are a number of paternity tests revealed on these shows. Talk about deception and lies!. The show sees that paternity tests are done, and are done for free. There are a number of court shows that have come around and they are real-life shows and they have real-life judges deciding matters. Many of these matters concern relationships and they all help to give people guidance. Judge Lynn Toler hosted *Divorce Court*. Divorce is obviously covered and, quite often, paternity tests are done on that show. These kinds of shows are educational and can be helpful to people who are married or about to be married. Judge shows were gradually given more TV slots than talk shows were.

What becomes obvious with some of the men on these judge/court shows is that they'd say they weren't the father or didn't think they were for as long as they could so they could avoid paying child support. In many cases, it was quite obvious what they were doing. They'd throw in all kinds of reasons and wouldn't believe the woman (or acted like they didn't). Then, when the paternity test proved they were the father (after they'd avoided child support and sometimes for years and years), they'd act surprised and be apologetic. So how many years had they sidestepped paying child support...? But, it wasn't just certain of the men who were full of pretense. With some of the women on these shows, they knew the child could be some other man's but they would act, vehemently, like the man on the stage with her was the father, when she knew he might not be or, in some cases, couldn't be the father. You realize how common in the world telling lies is. (Doesn't it say in the Bible, somewhere, that liars won't get into to Heaven...? There is something noted about lying in all world religions.) Some of the men and women on these shows may not have been lying, however.

It can never be good in any relationship to tell lies and let lies stand. You can just be silent about some things, or only give out a little information, but do not tell out-and-out lies. You can even slant things your own way, but do not tell any out-and-out lies. If you take the high road and work hard at your relationship and are faithful to it, what will you have to lie about? Deception only leads to distrust.

Other more eclectic judge or court shows that have touched on relationships from time to time have been headed by the following judges— Joe Brown, Mablean Ephraim, Alex Ferrer, Glenda Hatchett, Faith Jenkins, Mills Lane, Maria Lopez, Greg Mathis, Marilyn Milian, Karen Mills-Francis, Cristina Perez, Penny Brown Reynolds, Kevin Ross, Jerry Sheindlin, Judy Sheindlin, Frank Caprio, and David Young. Not all are still around (and there's been new ones, too). There was also a United Kingdom Judge Robert Rinder, seen on American television. More continue to enter the scene. Not all the cases are about relationships, just some cases are. One court show that came on the scene in the mid-2010s, *Hot Bench*, was based on one of the Irish court format-types having a three-judge panel, and so the show presented three collaborating judges—Patricia DiMango, Tanya Acker, and Larry Bakman. There was also the married pair of judges, the Cutlers (Dana and Keith), and their court show.

Like talk shows, court shows seem to come and go because they are very popular. Some stay around for a long time. They're quite instructive. Some of them deal with marriage and divorce and some of them deal with paternity. Some deal with more general, mainstream issues (Cases). Court shows seem to be here to stay. In one court show titled *Paternity Court,* relationships were the core of it but not all court shows can exclusively be relationship shows. Certain of the relationship talk shows are no longer on the air, either. Most stayed around for a long time. *Dr. Phil* has been very popular.

Kathy S. Thompson, M.A.

On the subject of judge shows, included is *Judge Jerry* and the judge is the infamous Jerry Springer. People were surprised when they saw him on TV as a judge. They hadn't even known he'd gone to law school, and so how could he suddenly have a judge show? Seeing that he was a judge was a pleasant surprise to me. He doesn't handle too many divorcing situations, but he does handle many relationship squabbles, as do all judges. Many people on these judge/court shows were, or are in a relationship, which is one reason why they are so interesting. They enlighten people, relative to what to do and what not to do in a relationship so all aspects of a relationships can improve, or in some cases, terminate. The divorce and the paternity cases are helpful—sometimes beyond words—but the general relationship ones have been helpful as well.

Jerry Springer also hosted the relationship show, *Baggage*, which was on late-night. He had his own talk show as well, which tended to deal with relationships of all kinds. Considerable conflict was in these relationships. What was at the core of the relationships on his talk show, as you find with other talk shows, was conflict. Some talk shows interview guests and have a variety of guests and only, sometimes, deal with conflict. Other talk shows only deal with conflict relationships. Those are the tough ones. These shows even have large-sized guards on the platform so fighting people can be separated. Relationships can get very heated on these shows and in real life. Sex is sometimes a part of the anger. In fact, it often is. When relationships are filled with bitterness and anger, the sex will be off-course. It may have even stopped completely, in the relationship, all because of the conflict. Often, these relationships include infidelity. Some are triangle relationships. Sex isn't usually specifically mentioned on these shows, but it is at the core of the conflicted relationships . . . and sexual deprivation can relate to the overall frustration, particularly with certain of the cases. Sex is important to all relationships. So is fidelity. Quite often, one partner is not treating the other partner well. Sometimes, there is some kind of lack that may always be, or it can be, somehow, corrected or fixed. When it concerns talk shows, and judge shows, there is usually more to the relationships than is able to be covered on the shows but much still comes out, anyway.

Competition for air time keeps increasing. There's a great deal of talent and expertise out there, on many fronts. There are only so many time slots. The fact that there is so much overall competition in the world these days, made worse by the negative behaviors that are around, puts a strain on relationships, marriages, whole families, and the workplace. Many types of relationship shows are here to stay, for this very reason. People like the dating relationships reality shows now, for example. These kinds of shows somewhat buffer the negativity that is being seen because when people end out together at the end of a series, this is seen as being

64

positive and this buffers the negativity that is being seen elsewhere. TV shows like *The Bachelor, The Bachelorette,* and *Bachelor in Paradise,* for example, have been popular. There is, also, *Married at First Sight,* and it is about marriage but since the couples don't know each other when they get married, it is roundaboutly about dating because each newlywed has to make efforts to get to know the other person and to adjust to them. There are a few other shows featuring people getting married under such circumstances.

There was also a reality television series titled *Marrying Millions.* Couples thinking of marriage were featured. One of them was super wealthy; another one was not even close to being wealthy. This series showed how the several-featured couples overcame the problems that hit them. With the couples, there could be a significant age gap, to boot. As you watched the show, you wondered, will they marry or won't they? The dynamics of the different relationships varied. Personalities and values were different. All these kinds of shows can help to improve the relationships that viewers have with other people so they are really self-help reality shows. Some don't stay around too, very long, though (like this one didn't).

Another TV series centering on marriage, or the possibility of marriage, *90 Day Fiancé,* was also extremely interesting to watch—start to finish—because two people come together (and there are quite a few couples) and one person is American and the other person is from a different country (like from Europe, South America or Central America, Africa, or the Middle-East). The relationship goes on, in America and the other country so film crews do considerable travelling. Each couple is always concerned about getting papers in for a K-1 Visa for the one person and they are concerned about getting in the right paperwork to be able to be married. Some couples end out having weddings in both countries. There are other Visa types they are sometimes concerned with, too. The Visas have deadlines (time allotments). There's the CR-1 Visa and a Spousal Visa.

This show has depth as do many Extension Shows that relate to it and are produced because of it (but will have different names or titles). The couples, technically, have ninety days to choose to be married or go through with a marriage (hence, the name of the series). After one episode is shown, another show related to the series—*Pillow Talk*—comes on and it is a commentary show. People talk about the different couples on *90 Day Fiancé* and the situations each couple is in, since all the situations are different. *Pillow Talk* is funny in places, plus it adds insight to each episode because much of what each individual on these shows does is discussed by a number of couples on *Pillow Talk.* The couples (or pair-ups) somewhat became celebrities. Certain ones especially had the gift of gab.

There are quite a few couples on *90 Day Fiancé* and there seems to have been some different follow-up shows for certain of the couples. One of them is *After the 90 Days*. Three others are *The Other Way*, *B90 Strikes Back*, and *Darcey and Stacey*. All of these spin-offs have couples whereby one person in the couple is from a different country besides the USA. These relationships are all extremely interesting because of the other-country aspect, and because of all the travel, too. The periodic commentary about the couples adds considerably to the different episodes. When watching these shows, professionals in related fields can build on their professional knowledge.

Ideally, watching these kinds of shows causes viewers to want to improve themselves, and to be of constructive help to their own partner and to their own family members. These kinds of shows can help to strengthen relationships. To a large extent, viewers can ascertain what they shouldn't be doing, or shouldn't have done. Ordinary every-day people are seen on these shows. Some parts are guided by show producers/directors, and there is acting and some over-dramatization, but behaviors and actions seem more real than otherwise and viewers can relate to that which seems real and is real. Viewers can get to where they feel they know the people on these shows, personally, which is one reason why viewers can learn so much from observing these kinds of shows. They can become very involved, when watching such shows.

Reality shows are really self-improvement shows . . . or they have the potential to be, depending on the particular viewer. They have not had many gay couples— only a couple of them, but they are starting to trend. Quite a few of the couples are mixed-race couples. Some of the couples do get married, and some end out having children. They all struggle—sometimes enormously. The relationships and their related problems are what are highlighted. Sex always relates to the quality of a relationship but sex is not covered all that much. Viewers are left to assume. It weaves through, some, though. It is the relationships that have the emphasis. These kinds of shows always relate to relationships and all the relationships vary. Not one is the same. Relationships are as snowflakes. Each composition will be different. All people are different, so relationships will be different.

These shows are most informative when it comes to sex trends and general relationships in America and in various other countries. Viewers' eyes get opened, relative to all kinds of issues. All the differences and the problems are quite interesting. With reality show scripts, it <u>seems</u> there is no scripting and that all the talking is impromptu but there is guided scripting in several places. Lines are totally read, or the featured people are told in advance not only what to say, but also what to do. More and more, certain reality shows have gone in this direction. It is very possible the featured people know, in advance, some of what they are to do and expect, even before they sign a contract with the show. Still, there is enough reality in these shows to cause them to be generally impromptu and, therefore, real.

Some relationships on these TV shows have occasional toxic elements, and it is interesting to see how the problems are worked through. There are times when viewers might see too much toxicity and doom in a certain relationship and so they aren't cheering for the relationship. Some relationships in life can be toxic, and usually one person in the relationship ends out suffering.

Some relationships start off good but end out bad. In one case I covered, a woman jumped in a little too fast and found out that the man she was seeing had sadistic streaks and enjoyed it when he hurt her and let her down. He was a very good-looking man and that is what first attracted her to him. This man also had homosexual leanings because he preferred the company of men, to an excess. He did not have respect for women, in general, and he may have even been a woman hater and he needed some counseling, for sure, because he wanted to stay in the relationship. Fortunately for her, the two were not married, nor did they end out having any children together. After a period of time, when all her observing and reviewing had been completed, the woman realized that the man was not even close to being the man for her. He wasn't really the man for any woman—not at the time— because he was abusive. He secretly wanted to be with a man so he resented this woman but he never completely went the homosexual route. He was in a confused state. Later on, the woman who he ended out marrying ended out reporting him two times for being abusive, and he went to jail for it. Then, his wife died. He, thereafter, got into a fight with a roommate and was reported to the police again because of physical assault and losing his temper. He'd had issues and had needed regular counseling. He had only been partly committed to counseling.

The man had a problem with self-control and he lacked love. He'd been somewhat of a body builder. He wasn't well liked at work, either. He was disrespectful to customers, which eventually got him in trouble. Over the long haul, he'd been too self-absorbed. He saw women with tunnel-vision. To him, they were one-dimensional, not multi-dimensional. He had made a conscious decision to disrespect women. He did not make the world a better place. Many men are like this, even some gay men are, but it is usually those younger who can be like this, and, many gay men aren't even close to being like this. They are not abusive.

Always check a person out when you first meet him (or her). Looks aren't everything. Neither is personality, necessarily. Neither is what someone does for a living, necessarily. Be careful. You do not want to become a statistic. Some women have ended out with men who have money, only to end out being abused and miserable. Just because a man has money does not mean he is a good man. Some men can be controlling and very selfish. They play life and relationships like they would a football game—rough and tough—and in truth, that is not the way life and relationships should be perceived and handled. Everyone has to get through life, everyone works and should be appreciated, everyone needs co-operation to be around them and should, themselves, co-operate.

Again, though, women have to allow men a certain amount of space and, at times, give them even more space than what they, themselves, have or wish to take. It's only right. It's only fair. Some men deserve to have more space than others do. We all know this. In a marriage, do not rob a man of enough needed space. Do not suffocate him or crowd the man out. Still and all, men aren't right about everything so women should take charge when they realize they must. It can all be a very fine line, and having enough wisdom when certain matters hit will certainly help. Life can be a struggle. It can be hit-and-miss and clarity is not always right there in front of you. Still, if a man doesn't deserve to have more space, he doesn't deserve to have more space. Women have to always draw from wisdom. Permissiveness isn't always the answer.

We can get into conjugal crime here, which includes wife-beating. Wife-beating or spousal abuse has been prevalent in society for some time. Wife-beating is not fair fighting. It is quite the contrary. When wife-beating occurs, the wife becomes fearful of the husband's superior strength and combative ability. She also becomes fearful of any weapons he has access to. A man can even be small, yet physically abuse his wife. Also, a small man can have access to a weapon. In any event, the wife is not able to match the man. His size, or temper, is too much for her. She cannot effectively defend herself or stop him from hurting her. Such a woman has not agreed to the abusive behavior, and furthermore, there may be no chance of reversal, postponement, discussion, or escape. The wife-beater seizes dominance, sets the rules, and at the moment of his anger, he intends to cause pain. He doesn't care enough about the wife to be controlled enough to stop himself. Also, drugs and/or alcohol may be in the mix.

Husbands who verbally threaten to kill their wives, as many abusers have done, may also threaten to kill their children. Twenty-five percent of all wife-beaters are white-collar workers, and the rest are obviously blue-collar workers (or unemployed). White-collar workers are those who have desk jobs and they don't all have a real-high income, though many do. They can be telephone laborers, for example, and take calls for companies and that would be considered white collar because they're sitting at a desk that is in an office (even if the office is a small cubicle). As becomes evident, one must be wary of compatibility factors that exist (or don't exist) before someone enters a marriage or even a relationship because beating and abuse may start off slight but it can escalate and end out tragically.

There can be reasons given, by the man, for the physical abuse, and some women may have pushed certain of the man's buttons, which caused him to explode (and she could have been doing this over a period of time), but no man should ever physically harm any woman. He needs to keep control of himself. He needs to figure out the best way to resolve issues. Harming someone is not an option and will not resolve anything. It will make things worse and bring about some additional problems. Consider finding a course in Anger Management somewhere, if you cannot keep your temper under control. Counseling will help all involved parties, though, so do not overlook counseling, even if it is only once a week, or even once a month. Some will even come in once every two or three months. Some counseling is better than no counseling.

When there is thoughtful discipline, men are supposed to be protectors of the home, as they tend to be protectors of the country, militarily. True, some women are now in the Military, but before not too long ago, it had always been men who were at the front, militarily. Even today, not too many women actually end out at the front, militarily. Women (and children) are not supposed to need protection <u>from</u> the man, they are supposed to be protected <u>by</u> the man. Sadly, though, some women do not let the man protect the home and they misinterpret the man's actions and intentions. Their perspective is cloudy. Some women are contentious and cause contentious. Some women are resentful of the man's position. The truth is—men are men and women are women so let men be men and women be women when there is a disciplined traditional marriage, or even just a disciplined traditional relationship (versus what is non-traditional, which can also be disciplined but with a different orientation).

Women can be abusive, too—especially verbally. Women need to be careful about what they say and especially how they say it. Some women antagonize the man and very well know what they are doing. Men don't like to be punching bags. They'll take a punch here and a punch there, but they do not like to get too many punches. Yes, inform. Yes, instruct. Yes, repeat when necessary. Yes, remind. But women have to be careful about nagging, harassing, needling, badgering, and criticizing men in general, and this would include not just their husband or significant other, but all men. Like women, men need to have validation, acceptance, approval, and respect. If these positives get overly eroded, there will be problems.

Certain men can, for sure, be a little less curt, rough, rude, and brutish when they talk to women, though, and that is something certain of them need to work on. Some men, quite frankly, deserve to look and be seen as offensive to women.

They're too corrosive and abrasive. They think wrong thoughts about women. With some men, sometimes exposure and shame is what is needed to get them to stop doing what they are doing. Quite a few well-known men, for example, have made the national News because of their bad treatment of women. Shame can change a person. It can bring a person to humility so they are more willing to see and admit their wrongdoing. It can cause people to turn to a loving God. Many say that God will chasten those He loves so they will see the light and change. Men can be stiff-necked and prideful and some of them need to fall flat on their face before God, very frankly.

Wife-beating and even brow-beating, which is verbally intimidating the wife into submission or acquiescence, relates to the inability to effectively communicate and to fight fairly and effectively at the right times and in the right ways. Often, the wife-beater or brow-beater is not real highly intelligent, but a few can be. The wife-beater or brow-beater is overly forceful and most of the time is unreasonable. He's this way with his kids, too, if he has any. This kind of man uses threats and intimidation to get what he wants out of his wife, which would include sex. Sex can become 'as rape'. This kind of man can become a rapist, as well as a wife-beater or brow-beater, but he never gets hauled in to jail for rape. He overtakes his wife, by using some kind of pressure, force, or intimidation and where can the poor woman go? If she doesn't want to have sex, it is too bad for her. No woman wants to have sex with a bully. Women respond to gentleness and acceptance because, again, they are nurturers. They respond to strength but it has to be the right kind of strength.

Wife-beaters have a distorted view of masculinity, usually. They are not good at handling normal relationships with people, in general, because they're off-balance and have gap areas in their life—gaps that need to be filled in, one way or another. Again, I write extensively about gap areas in my book, *Crime and Rehabilitation and the Gap Theory for Mental Assessment and Treatment*. The Gap Theory is a new one and I developed it so it would be both comprehensible and useable in several kinds of counseling settings. It does not just relate to crime and criminals. It can relate to anyone and everyone. The Gap Theory is thoroughly presented and explained in the book. The Gap Theory can be useful, relative to both men and women, and it can be applied to any number of professional situations.

A good book, and a very famous one, which was originally written by G. Bach and P. Wyden back in the 1960s, is titled *The Intimate Enemy*. The book thoroughly reveals and teaches how a couple can go about fighting fairly in their marriage and how they can express anger effectively without things getting out of hand. The book helps married people acquire skills for use when communicating. Education is a very effective weapon against negative things that could get out of hand in a marriage because Education teaches individuals how to go about managing their problems and their differences and it teaches people how to manage both conflicting and non-conflicting issues and situations on time. When a couple can handle frustration competently—both separately and together—they can become closer as a couple and then they will become more intimate. They will be able to build trust through understanding.

There are many self-help books out there, for both men and women. Women tend to read more of these types of books than men do but more men need to realize the value of these books and to start reading them. Men should <u>want</u> to hang out with women who are on a self-help path. Some of it will rub off on them. Women would rather see the man they love reading a self-help book than they would like to receive flowers or candy from the man, especially if there has been conflict and discord between them. Many self-help books can be of help, relative to a couple's existing problems. Go to a library or a bookstore and pick out those that seem to relate to whatever the problems are, but not all self-help books are direct or on a particular topic. Still, one that seems indirect might be a really helpful self-help book so don't overlook any of the self-help books.

In some cases, a self-help tape or even DVD can be useful. Allow all of these into your life—maybe not as a steady diet, but on occasion they will provide good ideas and guidance. To emphasize, if some particular problem is pressing down on someone, they should go to the library or a bookstore, browse, and pick out whatever looks helpful. Frankly, some of these books, tapes, or DVDs actually need to be <u>studied</u>, so the content is well grasped. If a man or woman would do this, their partner or spouse would probably be impressed. Both in a relationship can read, listen to, or watch the same exact book, tape, or DVD, and then they can discuss what they were exposed to. Just knowing that the other person realizes what the other person is realizing can be bond forming and strengthening.

# Chapter 7

# Intimacy, and Outside Relationships

In a marriage, good intimacy involves a two-way effort between the husband and the wife. The partners know each other as they are (which includes their shortcomings) and yet they have no fears about the relationship and do not have to play games with each other since they are each genuinely accepted by the other as being a person who has good times and bad, and highs and lows. Intimacy implies that there is no place to emotionally hide from a partner. It also implies that there should be no reason to hide. Intimacy is a warmly, personal 'being together' that is characterized by self-disclosure and affection. Intimacy is the experience of close, sustained familiarity with another person's inner life.

When you have this quality of intimacy, you are more apt to have fidelity in the marriage. Fidelity must, of course, be reciprocal. Some couples have more intimacy in their marriage than other couples have, but as long as there is enough intimacy, the marriage is all-right. Sometimes intimacy ebbs and flows in a marriage. Consistency of intimacy is always best, though, because during the 'ebb times' a marriage can be weak and even in danger.

Intimacy takes time and work, especially at first, before two people can get their foundation established. After that and all along the way, the couple must guard what they have. They must guard their foundation, against their own selves and against others and outside circumstances. The song, *You and Me Against the World,* can be a reminder that the couple must insulate their intimacy and their marriage from outside forces that could and do come in and can cause a weakening or a tearing apart of the marriage. The couple must realize what they have together and recognize its value. They must fight to not allow their relationship to be taken away from them or to get out from under them.

Each partner must be fair and gracious towards other people, though, and not see every person who is a part of their life as being a threat or an enemy and as being a potential danger to their marriage. Such defensiveness would be abnormal paranoia and it would generate its own set of problems. One can be intelligently guarded, to preserve their marriage, but one shouldn't be overly guarded and alienate good people (people who could actually benefit or help the marriage in some way). For example, some mothers and mothers-in-law have been treated unfairly and disrespectfully because one or both of the marrieds are prideful, selfish, and lack understanding. They can also lack maturity. These older women deserve to have space and to be a part of the couple's world, but some of them get shut out, and even treated badly. This is not right. Some young people take being on their own and being their own person a little too far.

Many outside people have to be a part of a married couple's world and some of them should be treated like they are very much wanted and valued guests. Too many good, well-meaning mothers and mothers-in-law get hurt and may not be fully accepted or accepted at all. This can be because of foolishness and selfishness on the part of young people who evaluate matters too narrowly and are not good at communication. These older women are sometimes irreparably hurt by a married couple's cold and unaccepting ways. True, a wife is now the husband's main focus and vice versa, and the two have become one and have left home, but is that any reason to snub, be rude to, and be unaccepting of a mother or mother-in-law? Many such women do not deserve the unkind and unfair treatment that has come their way because of younger married people. I've seen this happen all too often, by one or both partners in the marriage. Sometimes, there is unfounded resentment towards a mother or mother-in-law.

Sometimes, young people erroneously see a mother or mother-in-law as interfering, when the mother or mother-in-law is only trying to help and is hoping that her experiences and ideas will matter to the two younger people. Early in their marriage, too many young people are self-centered and want all the attention to go to themselves. They don't want to listen to an older woman even when they know that the older woman knows a lot. They can cause the older woman considerable unhappiness, sometimes for years and years and even to that woman's death. Many fathers and fathers-in-law get shut out, too, and don't deserve to be. Much relates to negative pride on the part of the young people, and too much insensitivity. Common courtesy goes out the window.

Marrieds can leave home to start a new home and family but they can, nonetheless, still make efforts to be on good terms with parents and in-laws. They can benefit from all that parents and in-laws have learned from their own experiences. They can still make their own decisions. It's as simple as that. Of course, it's also bad when one spouse or partner hangs on too tightly to a parent, and that can also happen. It's less common to hang on too tightly to a parent or an in-law, but this does happen. Usually, though, there is some kind of undeserved alienation that gets directed towards parents and in-laws, which, more often than not, should not be. It can actually be quite cruel.

The young wife is not older and wiser than the mother or the mother-in-law. Too many young wives wrongly decide to be resentful of the older women, and they are unkind and unfair when they allow themselves to be this way. They say bad things about the mother or mother-in-law to their friends and/or co-workers, if they work, just to make themselves feel more important and more in control. They don't look for the good. They don't want to see the good. This can be crushing to the mother or mother-in-law, who did nothing but be herself and did not deserve the negativity or rejection. This type of outlook and attitude applies to the young men, too. Young men want to be in control of their home and they do not want to rely on their father or father-in-law because they want to get control and sustain control. They want to have and sometimes even crave having their own space. They will hog the space and take away the space of older people when they aren't ready to and don't deserve to. They let ego block what is fair and best. Quite often, they just aren't honest about situations. They don't look at things quite right. Their selfishness and even fears get the better of them, at the expense of the older man, who did not deserve to be the brunt of a negative and oppositional attitude. Granted, older people are not always perfect but they are usually around twenty to twenty-five years further along in life (on average) than these younger people are.

All younger people should back off and be more respectful of older people. It used to be this way. It still could be this way, much more than it presently is because young people have had that much longer to experience this and that and to mull over what they are learning or have learned. True, when they marry, young people are to leave home and cleave to their spouse, but that doesn't mean they have to forfeit their relationships with older people, especially their parents. They're still younger than those older people are. They always will be.

Even though there may be exceptions, in-laws are actually very valuable and should be liked, respected, and treated well. Frankly, young people should humble themselves and admit this or at least try to go with a better flow. They, themselves, may choose to see the older people as threats but this is the wrong outlook and perspective. Why go about hurting blood relatives? You could be alienating them for life. If you were to realize twenty or more years later that you were wrong in your outlook and behavior, how will that help the blood relative now, during times when they are being hurt and suffering disappointment? Look at how much time and money they put into raising you when you were younger. Does that mean nothing to you? Why can't you humble yourself now and accept their worth and usefulness and treat them well and respectfully? Even if the older people have made some past mistakes, they most likely have learned from them and their mistakes are behind them. They probably have a roster of learnings now, because of their mistakes. Furthermore, they can pass on what they've learned to the younger people. For example, people who lived during the Viet Nam War and during the time when drugs got their start and got entrenched (in several countries) made mistakes then because it was a time of temptation, and disorientation and confusion. Young people now, if they had lived back then, would have made the same or at least similar mistakes. Some of these young people are making even more mistakes today; they're just different mistakes. Today is a time of disorientation, and conflicting values.

People need to overlook the mistakes of others because time does heal and can change things (sometimes a lot more than is realized). People learn and grow. Too many people don't overlook the mistakes and imperfections of others, regardless of the times when they occurred. Because of their own selfishness and ego, they won't allow themselves to see the bigger picture. Everyone makes mistakes. Everyone errs, or as the theologian would say "sins". No one is perfect. Find the good in people and discipline yourself to say no to yourself when you are about to reject a generally good person. Let them have some space. Share space with them. Sometimes even give them all the space. Why not, if they deserve it. All people need some space from time to time so they can be happy, feel good, have dignity, thrive, feel like they're contributing something and are of value, and so they can focus in on their work and daily activities. Realize this, about others, and about yourself. Be willing to share and to give. Let some things roll off your back. Don't be a hog.

Sadly, one person in a couple may see a mother-in-law as being pushy, which can be a totally wrong word to use. The mother-in-law may just be being enthusiastic. She may just be being talkative, and may have no motive, whatsoever, about what she is saying. She may just be trying to bless other people's lives as she goes along. At the same time, she may but have any expectation that any or all of her views will be heeded or agreed to. The very last thing such a woman is, is a meddling busybody, but a young person having less insight and experience might choose to see it that way. (This can also apply to fathers-in-law.) Too many young people misperceive things, and then alienate themselves from good people. Then, if they see the errors of their ways later on, they may choose to not apologize because of their own pride and ego. They still want to hog space, not share, or give out any space.

Frankly, in this day and age, older people generally just present their views and figure 'come what may' because they know that other people can think for themselves. Older people know that people around them are all at different places of development and growth—emotionally, intellectually, and spiritually. They realize that what they say will be as a smorgasbord anyway. They know that everyone has free will. They aren't being augers or brow-beaters. Even if some people seem a little pushy, it is often because they have already learned something and don't want the young person to make the same mistake(s) or be in error. They are trying to help, because they care.

If everyone would love and accept one another, and keep arrogance, high-mindedness, and fears out of the picture, there would be many benefits for all concerned. Let the older relatives—all of them—have some deserved space. Don't make excuses to not. Also, keep some space for yourself. If you are married or in a secure relationship, accept everyone's gifts and qualities. Love both sides of the family—faults and all. Love people in the family, regardless of their age. Don't allow yourself to be resentful of anyone. Frankly, you are not first and best, in a family. You are a co-contributor. There may be a few people who you could dislike, but why not make an effort to tolerate them and be civil and even polite, even if they may do you wrong. Even give those people some space, and most certainly, don't go around trying to one-up older people.

Families need one another and not just superficially. Many families do not have solidarity. Solidarity or unity can be and is often feigned. If young people have harmony with the older people in the family, the couple will tend to have better, more loving sex, not sub-standard or less-involved sex. Sex can sometimes be neurotic-based, and it can be empty, too, if something isn't right. When there is more intimacy, there will be more involvement during sex. Sex will be better.

You don't have to give the older relatives a great deal of space, just give them enough space. Let them take a little of yours—why not? Be fair and honest. Don't cheat older people out of the space they deserve. They've gone before you. A generation makes a big difference. Just think about that. Two generations make even more of a difference. Include older people in your life, and try to be kind and respectful to them. Be good to grandparents and other older people.

Again, older people, generally, have learned some good lessons along life's path so talk to them and get to know what makes them tick and be respectful when you are around them. Never turn on them. Younger people will have gaps in their life that the older people won't have so many, but the younger people will not realize that. Young people should never design and try to one-up older people, like so many young people do today and 'know not what they do' (or do they, because at times, they probably do know what they are doing). At the very least, young people should be level and civil, and not hurt or upset older people by one-upping them.

Also, they should never one-up older people around other people. Some young people will do this and who are they to do such a thing? That, in essence, is abusive. It is morally wrong to do that. When the young person gets to be the older person's age, years down the road, which will happen to them, they may then see the folly and foolishness of their previous action or actions but they can never make restitution or amends because the older person will probably be dead. Too many years will have gone by. The damage done will have remained for years, too, while the older person had been alive. Such behaviors contribute to the older person's lack of happiness. Was it really worth it to do something so wrong? Some behaviors are as negative demerits.

You can accept the older people in the whole, extended family, and still make your own decisions. You can include all the older people in your life, be around them, and even enjoy being around them. Just come to an agreement, early on, to not let strife in and to not allow yourself to be unaccepting of the contributions that the older family members have to offer. Why would you want to shut them out? You are not their age yet, so you know more than they do? You've been as many places in life as they've been? You've done as many things, thought as many thoughts, and lived as many days? They are counting on you to love them and to accept and include them. If you hit on a point of controversy when talking with older people, you're your own person. You don't have to get all bent out of shape, resentful, and disagreeable just because you don't agree with someone who is older. Assert yourself in a generally polite way, relative to your idea or view. State your reasons and then put it all aside. Don't start an argument and try to show the older person up. Stay respectful but move on—by changing the subject, or leaving. Use some humor. That sometimes works. You could actually be wrong, too, and won't be able to realize that any time soon.

Too many people are prideful and always want their own way and do not want to accept that older people have been around longer than they have been. If you can, find out why the older person thinks what they think before you end out leaving or changing the subject. Listen and think about what they said. Don't gloss over their ideas. Don't minimize their efforts and contributions. A little appreciation goes a long way. Remember, you will always be younger than they are. When you say your piece, be at peace. Also realize that young people have a lot to contribute, too; they always do. Mainly, be respectful of those who are older. Treat them well.

Keep strife and contention away from you, in general, and from your relationship with your spouse or partner. Anyway, in a discussion, people don't have to be right or wrong because they're in process of learning from the discussion and extending on their thinking from what all is said during a discussion. This is how personal growth is benefited. Then, there's always the statement "your ideas are very interesting; I'll think some more about the subject but I don't have any more to add just now". Then, there's always "I don't have an opinion about that". Both statements are stoppers. And both are fair ways to end a conversation, for everyone. There are other statements that could be made, too. Be wise, tactful, and kind. Use your intelligence when you are communicating—always. Don't be a sloppy communicator and say whatever you want. Be careful about what comes out of your mouth.

It can be a challenge to handle difficult and opposing people, wherever they are and whoever they are. Some people can be off-the-mark, negative, and difficult. When you get to the point where you can deal with such outside people, you will then be able to handle strife and problems in a relationship considerably better, because you've developed your communication skills. There can be 'nice' opposition. In other words, there can be opposition using manners, and disagreeing can be done with a smile. It can all come about by way of friendliness. What was thought to be opposition in the 1950s and 1960s was light compared with what all goes on today. What all goes on today in the way of flack, rudeness, and opposition can be quite flagrant, harsh, and all too incessant. Rudeness and harshness, when it is open and obvious and clear opposition, can be startling because it is so nervy. It can come about fast. It can be very difficult to handle that kind of opposition when you've been in the right and the opposing person is doing you wrong or is in the wrong. In fact, such behavior can rather stun you and you can be taken aback. You can hardly believe what is happening. This kind of communicating should not be happening in a marriage.

On the other hand, is hard to not be nice towards some opposing person who is being nice. You pretty much have to just walk away, even if you are upset. What can you do? There are options. You can turn around and confront the person and show the person that you're upset. You can go with the flow and pretend that all is okay. You can walk away and have no more contact with the person for the time being. You can change the subject. You can have a continued discussion with the person and point out the obvious problems and present your point of view (which would probably be best, if they'll hear you out). You could even send the opposing person a letter that expresses your views. Or, you can keep letting the person oppose what you think and believe, which, really only hurts them if they are wrong. Still, always keep in mind that there are times when silence is golden. It is easier to converse with nice people than it is to converse with combative people.

There are toxic people out in the world and even in one's own family. Purposely try to have conversations with people in your life so you can determine who is toxic.

You can tell how they react whether they are toxic or aren't. You can tell, by what they say. If they lack compassion when it is more than evident that they should show or reveal some compassion, then that could well be a rather evident sign that the person is toxic. If they gossip unmercifully about people who don't deserve to be gossiped about to the extent that they are and in the way that they are, then that person is most likely toxic. If the person is not 'other-person' oriented and is all too often a 'me, myself, and I' person, then they are probably toxic. If the person constantly cuts people off from expressing themselves, interrupts (versus interjects) way too often, then that person is likely toxic. There are signs. Still, even toxic people can change and you may be able to help change them so converse with them and try to love them. However, their changes may be slow to come and plus, they may not listen to you. Toxic people can change, but you don't know when or even if they will change. All you can do is mark them as being definitively toxic and proceed with caution whenever you are around them. Probably don't tell them all that much. Keep a bit of a distance from toxic people. Again, they could change, so be looking for a change. Then again, they may never change one bit, so don't be disappointed if they don't.

Some people today are getting the jitters when and if they have to be around other people, regardless of who those people are. They have a social phobia and don't like to encounter even one person and certainly more than one person. They have approach-avoidance conflict all the time. Some don't even like to leave their home or talk on the phone. And why are more and more people becoming like this? Because the people they keep encountering are rude and high-minded and continually one up them. People are becoming more manipulative and grabby, too. The world has become unpleasant because of all the usurpers and one-uppers, or, at least, because of all the people who continually make efforts to try to one-up others. They don't always succeed because people stand up for themselves or see through the charade, but, why should the defenders even be put in the position of having to stand up for themselves? They never did anything wrong in the first place but still got one-upped.

Probably, more Manners classes should be taught in the schools, starting in elementary school. Manners should be part of all school curriculums, starting in elementary school, and going through to both junior high, and high school. Furthermore, it would be great if Manners was offered in colleges and universities, at least as an elective. I'm not sure what department it could be taught under, though; maybe it could be tied in, somehow, with two or three different programs?

Again, when it comes to how some people treat other people, why do people have to go around acting like they're little gods and goddesses? There's this 'I'm superior' mentality in all too many people and as a result, there is a corresponding mistreatment of many people and that would very definitely include older people. Certain younger people today even tend to mistreat older people and psychologically abuse them. Only some of these older people stand their ground. Some turn the other cheeks for a number of reasons (they may be tired, for one thing), but their wisdom is always at the helm. Sometimes, older people aren't treated well in nursing homes by the younger staff. Many times they are treated well, or at least all right. Such homes can also be understaffed.

Young people should go and visit any older relatives who are in a nursing home. Older people get all but forgotten all too easy. Write to them regularly, if the older relatives live far away. Don't wait for a response. Keep writing them. Let them know you care about them and let them know how you are doing so they do not feel so alone. More of the younger people, in general, should go around and visit old folks' homes, even if they are visiting strangers, but you usually have to give a reason to the main office for visiting them. Some old folk's homes are closed to allowing strangers to come in, unless they are teaching a class or bringing in some kind of Show and Tell, like bringing in stamps, coins, rocks and minerals, or seashells, etc.

Keep in mind that anyone in a marriage can end out in a nursing home. Sometimes, one person in the marriage has to actually put the other person in the marriage into a nursing home. This can happen when a situation becomes extremely difficult and there is no other recourse. This can happen against the other person's will and there can be fierce opposition. Older people do not want to leave the safety and comforts of their home. So often, too, they have shared love and life with the person they are being forced to leave, which makes things even harder. This kind of unhappy separating happens after people have been married for many years. They likely had equal commitment to the other, in that they had been married for a long time. This kind of unhappy experience can happen in old age, but many older people are able to live at home, and will die at home.

Fighting can occur regardless of the ages of two people in the marriage. Fighting fairly in a marriage can be extremely challenging. It's never good to hit below the belt because that is unfair fighting. Calmness and intelligent thought are good. If certain infractions keep happening, over and over, it can be hard to stay calm. Anyone can reach their limit with another person. When you are married you have to stay open to what the other person in saying and listen to what they have to say. You have to try to be accommodating whenever possible and as often as possible. You may even have to give in at times. (Some things just aren't that important). When something is important, you might want to write down your points before you enter into a discussion or an argument. Take a little time out to do that, then get together. Strive for an effective discussion with your spouse, partner, or significant other at every bend and turn.

Make time to have a discussion with your spouse, partner, or significant other at many a bend and turn. A discussion achieves as much, or more, than an argument does. A discussion goes back and forth better and gives those involved a better chance to both process and retain the content that is being bantered about. Set a time for having a discussion, and it should not be when one or both is over-fatigued or under any kind of influence from alcohol or drugs (and as a reminder, excess alcohol and any drug use can easily destroy a relationship). Thinking and using logic is not at its best when the brain is being affected by alcohol or drugs. Choose the best time when important matters can be discussed so that thinking will be lucid and behavior will be better under control. All couples 'discuss' and all couples 'argue'. Everyone expressing their view needs to go about it more thoughtfully and caringly and stay within a certain range of emotion.

In life, not everyone wins, prevails, or succeeds at everything they try to do. Today, there are some rather conspicuous sore losers who demonstrate spite to an excess and become a bad example to other people. Something is horribly lacking in, at least, some of these sore losers. So often, it is even illogical to be a sore loser, especially to the point where a person does off-the-wall, strange, whacko, crazy things and ends out shooting way off the bulls-eye. Many, on the other hand, will just move on in a generally quiet and no-fuss way. Some will even turn the other cheek and do not make a big deal out of losing, in any way, shape, or form. They don't become fault-finders. They don't make a bunch of excuses. They aren't retaliatory.

In a marriage, be very careful about becoming a sore loser (or an arrogant, smug winner). But, no one in a marriage should really be a loser or a winner. Marriage should not be looked at that way. There should be no competition, in other words, and no contesting. It is more like you are on a baseball team, together, than if you are two players on opposing sides or teams. Still and all, there will be some disputing and fighting in a marriage. It is inevitable. If you are a sore loser—openly or to yourself—you will carry, with you, a root of bitterness that can grow and fester. Somehow, that root has to be uprooted, and the only way to do that is by way of effective (and enough) communication and sometimes, by counseling. Do not allow yourself to lose the desire to communicate with your partner because that will be bad. Put enough effort into communicating so there will be an honest resolution, versus an artificial one. Try more than once to resolve conflict, obviously, if there is no resolution or if there is an incomplete resolution. Don't always be in a hurry to resolve conflict.

Ingredients for successful sexuality, then, are effective communication, fighting fair, building intimacy, taking time out to communicate (both sexually and otherwise), caring about other people (including parents and in-laws), and, being faithful within a marriage in various ways. With these positives being present in as much as is possible, a marriage will be considerably insulated and protected. When there are fewer arguments or when arguments are handled more diplomatically, all aspects of the relationship will be improved, including in the arena of intimacy.

Adding in some ideas about fidelity here, the most dangerous aspect of adultery or infidelity is that it involves being dishonest, when a good marriage requires honesty. Usually, cheating in marriage means that the other partner is cheated out of a 'consistently' satisfying sexual relationship. In essence, too, the cheating partner is saying to the other partner that they are looking for and hoping to find a better sex partner and partner in general—a partner that is perhaps even more intimate and sexual than the partner they presently have is. And so, when you think about it, why did the cheating person even marry the first person in the first place and why are they even staying in the marriage? The cheated-on partner is obviously not enough for the cheating partner, and may never be. The two will need to talk this over and/or go in for counseling.

A marriage may have started out on shaky ground. A partner who is currently cheating should not really be permitted to have sex with their spouse because they essentially terminated the marriage by cheating. The cheating partner is forcing insecure feelings on their partner because that person feels that their partner is trying to find a better partner than they have been and are. They've really slapped their partner in the face and the partner certainly has the right to divorce the cheating partner. They may not have any alternative. Their partnership has been broken and may not be able to be repaired. Intimacy between the two people will just naturally become very poor. They dynamics will change. The person cheated on may feel repulsed. Certainly, they won't be able to feel all that loved. They will be sad, and will possibly have trust issues—then, and in the future. They will also be angry.

Some theologians say that God says that adultery is grounds for divorce. (The major God-centered religions believe this.) The unfaithful person has already left their partner in his or her heart and has either left in part or in full. They may still be in the same home but they aren't there emotionally for their partner—not really. They're in some far away land, in their thoughts. They are being manipulative. When adultery has occurred, the person who was cheated on is 'free to leave' because divorce (separation), in a roundabout way and in essence, has already taken place by the separating act of adultery. Adultery is a final act, whether it seems like it is or doesn't. Sometimes a partner will forgive a spouse for their infidelity, but regardless of the forgiveness, the hurt person is still free of the other person (before God) if they want to be free because the other person broke and essentially terminated the marriage vows. A couple can try going the renewed marriage vows route if there's been adultery, but this should only happen if there's been a complete turn-around on the part of the vow-breaker.

Many divorces come about because each person in the marriage doesn't get enough of what they want, and often of what they need. There may not be enough of what is needed. One person could be too much of a hog so everything is too one-sided. Also, outside issues and situations (and certain people) can be taking too much away from the relationship. All marriages are complex. All too often, one person isn't doing enough to share in the load; they really are not doing their part, when it comes right down to it. This can relate to household tasks or to marital effort, in general. Finally, the other person can't take it any more (and for good reason, usually). Yes, divorce happens because of poor communication, but communication can break down if one person is not doing enough, and not co-operating enough, too. The omission person (the person not doing their part or their share) will make excuses, and even find fault with the non-omission person, because of their complaining. The omission person can get stubborn and be unyielding because they want people to cater to them and to be able to continue in their ways. Their overall input can be much less than the other person's.

Principally, total love involves being faithful to the other person, in all areas and all of the time, so that when put to the test, faithfulness will over-ride temptations. A total love means that individuals will maturely hold to values that hold the marriage together, and not hold to ideas that will tear it apart. Tear-apart ideas would not be very safe. To be able to adjust to marriage, each partner needs to know themselves very well, and to accept themselves. Then they can face their own selves honestly, and look through facades, shams, and pretenses when and as they see them. When there is this transparent self, each person in a marriage can grow. It isn't a matter of humility—not per se. It relates to their having an inner drive to acquire self-improvement, to put negative and worthless things about themselves and their lives behind them, and to overcome their weaker and baser selves. Humility is good to have, too, though. A little humility can go a long way. We are not God. We are not as gods. We are but human.

# Chapter 8

## Commitment, Children, and Church

Responsibility for one's own life and for the life of the other person within the marriage or any strong relationship is a sign of maturity. Any blaming of the other person or using the excuse of bad luck to justify failure becomes more and more difficult to do as a person assumes his or her own responsibility and works to achieve a better life. When a person is more mature, that person can be entrusted with the responsibility of marriage, and also of raising children. Coming into the arena of maturity takes time and it doesn't happen in a day. Some people have children too soon, before they are mature and strong enough to handle parenting. Conversely, some couples don't have children early enough, at a time when they should be starting a family. This can be because of under-confidence, lack of faith and purpose, lack of money, a desire to put career or travel and adventure first, and sometimes because of selfishness. Poor planning can factor into the equation, too. Some couples spend too much money too fast—sometimes on themselves and for things they do not need. Then, they can't afford to have a baby. Young couples should buy used and not new items, for example, and also buy less. They should make an effort to live on less.

If one of the partners lacks stable integration (as a human being), then they will be imposing negative things on a child or on any children in the family. This will cause the child or the children some harm. Children need parents for a good many years and if an adult inside of a marriage isn't able to give children stability, then they have no right to start a family. It is only through constant, deep involvement in a child's life that a person becomes a true parent. Parenting is a serious issue, for all concerned. A person who lacks parenting essentials, however, can always step up to the plate and learn what those essentials are.

Would it not be good if child caring classes (or parenting classes) were required of all first-time parents and if they were sponsored, financially, by the government?

This could be made to be mandatory for pregnant women to complete such a course before they have their baby. Were such a program made to be mandatory, fathers would have to follow suit but they could take the course at a different time, and even on different dates. Possibly, so many hours of curriculum could be completed by both and if it weren't completed by a certain date, there could even be a fine? The course times could even initially be rescheduled, but not too often. Twelve hours total of training (or even more) would be good; then they would get a certificate. There would also have to be a practicum, or some acquired hands-on experience.

These parenting classes could take place at community colleges, local schools, convention rooms at centers or hotels, and even at restaurants, when they weren't open for business. Infant behavior, safety, sleeping habits, cleanliness and health needs, infant furniture, dressing, diaper (nappy) changing, bottles and feeding, breastfeeding, burping, holding and handling, etc., etc., could all be covered. Psychological aspects could also be explored and taught. Bonding with the infant could be but one feature of the course. There would be greater parent success, and less infant mortality, were such a program to be required.

Couples wanting to adopt children could also be required to take such a course, even if the children might be older; a different curriculum could be set up for them. No one would escape having to take this course; others (who were not yet having children) could even take the course, voluntarily; the teachers wouldn't have to be paid much, but they'd have a stable job. Establishing such a nation-wide course may not be feasible at the present time, but it could become feasible and be made to be feasible. A number of citizens would be grateful to have it available. Most everyone would, probably. It would be of such benefit to all children, and to the parents.

Some parents are not very good ones. A child needs to have both parents involved in a two-parent home because the child will take a parent's lack of involvement as rejection and they may live their whole life trying to win the approval and acceptance of that rejecting or all too-aloof parent, who probably doesn't deserve that child's time and attention because of their unfortunate lack of involvement and concern. Frankly, there are at least some parents who are never able to, or who never allow themselves to see their child or children as being important human beings. Their own importance comes about when they put their kids down and so they do. They never truly accept their children as being special and worthy. They make their kids unhappy, instead of happy. Any caring they may show is superficial. At least some people like this will have kids and this is most unfortunate. Such parents should take parenting classes, for sure, but really, all parents should.

Generally, parents get better with time but a structured program/course, early on, would give them a head start. I wrote a book on this very subject titled *The Equal*

*Personage Concept of Children and Youth* (EPCCY). The concept of equal personage is explained and expanded on, in this book. It is a concept that should be applied to parenting but also to many fields of work that involve children and teenagers. Education, Social Services, Criminal-Juvenile, Recreation and Parks, and Health and Welfare are just five of those fields. The book would tie in with any program that is adapted to children and teenagers. It was written for the mainstream; it is Education-oriented. It has been written to include for a number of fields but it has also been written for parents. The book would help parents early on and straight through, as they are raising children. It would improve their life, in general.

In today's world, parents don't usually bother with parenting classes, but in tomorrow's world, could the government require young parents to, at least, take a relatively short child caring course with only around twelve-hours of content? Such a course would be a help to <u>all</u> parents. Frankly, it sometimes seems that government does too much, relative to some things and not enough, relative to others. This course could easily be set up; it could easily be voted in. The curriculum would have to be a national-based or perhaps a state-based one, and participants could not miss one hour of the program. The course would have to be well structured and inclusive of essentials and perhaps some near-essentials. Lawmakers, are any of you reading this?

If two people cannot take childrearing seriously, they could cause their children to be emotionally ill and scarred. Their children will, then, end out being burdened with confusion. Obviously, these kinds of parents will not enjoy the years that they have with their children. Neglected children are not given the genuine focused attention that they need. Harry Chapin's song, *Cat's in the Cradle*, well illustrates this scenario. The song is older but it is still remembered. The words of the song reveal how a father can be too neglecting of his son because the father is too busy and doesn't make time for the son (when he could have if he had really wanted to). The father's ever visiting the boy becomes 'pie in the sky' for the boy. It doesn't happen. Then, the son grows up and does the same thing to his own son and the cycle continues. However, being too busy for a child because of a desire to work and earn money, or for whatever else could be the reason, is not as devastating to a child as it is when a parent constantly puts a child down, which can often continue until, by some change of circumstance, the son or daughter is able to get free of the oppressive bombardment of unkind bahavior. Leaving or escaping usually doesn't happen until the son or daughter is an adult and has to go out in life on their own. By that time, they are likely not in good psychological shape. They are damaged.

Brow-beating a child is more often done by a father. Hopefully, the mother will try to protect the child and smooth things over, but this is not always the case. If a parent is of this brow-beating inclination, they probably shouldn't have had children (depending on the severity of the brow-beating). Some brow-beating might be needed, on occasion, if the child is oppositional or simply isn't mindful. It might not really be brow-beating, in some cases. It might simply be disciplining. Words matter and it will depend entirely on what words are used, and also on each situation. How something is said can also matter.

To have children, and how many children to have, will need to be joint decisions. Today, people who like children enough to have them will want to share, with their partner, the satisfaction of watching a baby grow into a child, a child, into a teenager, and a teenager, into an adult. Agreement about raising children with consistent religious values, mutually shared, causes less confusion for a child and gives him or her an early foundation for belief and values that will make their adjustment to life easier and will create more harmony in their own homes, later on, assuming they marry someone of general like-belief.

In a relationship, like belief doesn't need to be exact but it does help considerably to have similar beliefs. It sets up a foundation for consistency and agreement. Decisions and actions of each partner will be more consistent, and more predictable. The more disagreements and opposing views that exist with a couple, the more frustration there will be. Some views can be more heated and contested, too. There are many good parents who do not share a belief or a faith with a spouse. Also, some may not take their religion that seriously. Some may rely on knowledge accumulation and intellectualism to see them through, when there are religious differences. Some may rely on personal philosophy and even political belief to see them through.

Relative to political belief, if two people are significantly polarized, there will be problems, rest assured. There will be constant friction and frustration. At times, there will be no acceptance, especially if one or both take politics seriously. There have been a few such relationships around, but there's going to be lacks in those kinds of relationships, no matter what anyone says. Such a couple could even die in old age at around the same time, but there will have been a feeling of isolation and aloneness that would have constantly surfaced over the years. That is what is logical, but it's a very sad situation for all concerned. Initially, politics may not seem that important, but political ideas and issues will come up and cause discord. Such marriages can be hard on the children, too. The two people just won't be of one mind.

Some don't feel that religion is important, but perhaps that is because no one has ever pointed out to them certain, positive advantages that there are when people hold to helpful and consistent beliefs. Religion can even be a primary unifying force in a marriage, to which all else can be subordinate. In America, in many homes, this is the case. Many people are religious. Going to church, a synagogue, or a mosque causes the two people in a marriage to become more alike in their thinking, to be in a constant state of self-assessment, and to grow and develop as individuals and as a couple within the boundaries of their church, synagogue, or mosque. Religion can strengthen families, if the right teachings are learned and applied. In the USA, there are not many synagogues or mosques in most localities, but churches are a different matter and there are many choices a couple can make. They can visit several churches, over the course of time.

Relative to churchgoers, wise choice concerning what church to go to is imperative. (There are churches and there are churches). Some couples visit several church types before they decide on one church type. A couple should end out attending a church that is in line with their predominant beliefs (at the time), or they aren't being true to themselves or to their God. Sometimes it takes visiting several churches before a couple finds the best church for them. It can take a few visits to even figure out what a church is teaching. If you are Jewish, you go to a synagogue. If you are Muslim, you go to a mosque. If you are Buddhist, you go to a temple. But if you are Christian, there are many types of churches you can visit or attend. You don't want to be too picky and particular, because no church is perfect, but, you want to generally feel comfortable about where you attend church. If you are going to give money to a church, to support the church, you want to know the church is for you. The church should be 'doing for others'. Synagogues, mosques, temples, and churches are as small neighborhoods, or communities. Sometimes a congregation is referred to as a family.

Concerning churches, many people end out going to a church that differs from what had been their initial inclination, relative to church attendance. Freedom of religion should always prevail. In many countries, it doesn't prevail and in fact, there is religious persecution. Sometimes it is horrendous. This goes on in many countries around the world. In the Western World, for the most part, people are free-will agents when it comes to choosing a religion. Often, people not only cross over to a different denomination, but they cross-over to a different religion, entirely. If it ends out that a spouse or partner is of a different religious persuasion, the two should try to consciously find some commonalities, because there probably are some. Christian and Jewish have commonalities; Catholic and Protestant have commonalities; Buddhism somewhat fits in with Jewish or Christian because of kindness teachings, but Jewish and Christian don't, really, fit in with Buddhism because there is a Jewish and Christian God; Muslim does not fit in with Jewish, Christian, or Buddhism because Allah is All-ah. He is all there and is for all their people. With Muslim belief, there is no room for the acceptance of the Jewish people's major and minor Prophets, and of Jesus as an extension of God and as God (i.e. as the Trinity).

Muslims are very intense about converting people, which is fine when they are in a free country that allows freedom of religion. Some Christian groups are thusly inclined, as well. The Jewish Faith does not go about converting people—not so much. In the main, Jewish people are part of a race of people; by marriage, outside people may convert. Before someone marries someone of a different Faith, they should do a study of both Faiths, and also learn about any history associated with both Faiths. They should talk about both Faiths with their intended before they marry, and even before they get engaged, assuming a formal engagement precedes the marriage, which it sometimes doesn't.

A successful marriage is broad in scope, and two people never stop adjusting to new situations that arise and they never stop growing as people. Commitment to each other and to the marriage is the umbrella of the marriage. The higher the commitment between the two, the easier it is for them to lay down roots, to derive security from their relationship, and to cope with life traumas and crises together. As a couple, the two people build, rebuild, and do not turn their backs on the other person when the other person needs them. Loyalty to the other person is of utmost importance—from start to finish. Often, faith-based people are, in their view, tested by God or circumstance or both and how they choose to look at these tests will be of significance and this is one reason why some people want to marry within their own Faith.

Life is not a bowl of cherries. Life is not a beach. It has its difficult times. Everyone is going to have stress and sorrow, and people are going to let other people down. When outside people let one person in the couple down and don't pick them up, figuratively speaking, the partner is the one person who should love them enough to pick them up and give them encouragement, no matter what the situation. You don't want to pat the partner on the back if the partner was clearly wrong about something, but you can still show love, give encouragement, and be there for the person. (There are kind ways to show disagreement.) An unconditional love for the other person should be present and it should always be willingly felt and present. It should not be contrived or feigned. Both partners have to decide that they will love the other partner unconditionally and at all times. It's something that must consistently be done and remembered to be done.

Money does not give satisfaction or love, per se. A dependable, loving, considerate, and helpful mate is probably one of the most hard-to-find treasures in the world today because people take each other and any prospective marriage too much for granted and do not appreciate the good qualities of other people—not in full. Not only that, but behaviors have become rude and high-minded, which can be hard to live with and be around. It's one thing to have to be around rude and arrogant behaviors as you 'go about town'; it's another thing if you have to be around it in your own home. Some people do not look for the good, often because they are too selfish and self-absorbed to want to see the good in others.

Some people's attitudes are not as high-level as they could be—towards their mates and also towards their children. Many people can't even have children and if they could, they wouldn't take them for granted like some parents do. There are many people waiting to adopt children, and some of these people are wealthy. They very much want a child. In many countries, more people want to adopt than there are babies and children available to adopt, but even if this weren't the case and there was an excess of babies, each and every child is a blessing and of value, no matter where they are in the world. None should be taken for granted and under-valued. (Somehow, Angelina Jolie comes to mind.) Some people go to other countries to find children to adopt but that is not always so easy to do. If people want a child, it's always good to look in to doing this, just in case it is feasible. First, the places to go to have to be found and then comes the visit—sometimes overseas. Then the problem can be—how do we get the child out of the country because doing this may not be so easy to do? A process will be involved.

Having children is a privilege, and abortion is a symptom of the mass confusion that exists in society. Children are additions to a couple's life and each child should be viewed as being a positive and a blessing. For those who hold to the Bible, their belief is that God designed man and woman anatomically and enabled them to, therefore, come together to create new life. In other words, man and women can procreate. When God made them, He did not want them to abort their own children. People who hold to this view believe that this makes sense. God did not make them so they would be unable to procreate, in other words. God designed the man and woman to fit together, sexually, and He made a woman so she would be able to biologically carry a baby and carry it to full term. God wanted a creation filled with people, in other words. If you believe in a more detached God or no God at all, you won't believe that way. The world, of course, has diversity. Some say God was lonely, and that He wanted human beings to be a part of His Universe. In the Old Testament, God said 'go forth and multiply', and we've been doing that ever since. Aborting children is not multiplying, it is subtracting.

Many women who had abortions are sad that they did. They can never get that baby back. They don't know where the soul of that baby is. Some women grieve the loss of their aborted babies later on and they will have a belated memorial service for the baby. Some do not get counseling in time, before making the decision to abort a baby. Later, they regret that they did not take time out to go in for counseling. Some women may not have even thought about counseling because they were under pressure. Some women are glad they had the abortion, at least for a while they are, but later on they realize that it wasn't the best decision that they could have made. Some women never get another chance to have a baby, and they can regret that they had an abortion for that reason, too. Some women just didn't get the guidance they needed, to encourage them to keep the baby.

Prior to having an abortion, some women will rationalize "well, others are doing it", "it's not really human yet, it's just a fetus", and "oh well, I can always have another one", but the day comes when they deeply regret their decision to abort and it is, then, too late. Some will acknowledge that the fetus was a human being, but, this notion of the fetus being a human being is opposed by many. This will continue to be a debated topic. Some girls and women do not take it so hard after they've had an abortion, and even later they don't feel badly; they see things differently than the more lamenting women do.

There has been much on the News about late-term abortion, which is the most controversial topic of all that centers on abortion, but the topic centering on whether or not the fetus is a human being is, really, just as controversial. Single women get an abortion. Married women get an abortion. The father of the child has a right to know if the woman carrying his child is considering having an abortion. This, too, has been debated, since what is involved is the woman's body, not the father's. If the woman has a close relationship with the father, he will not be happy if he is not informed before the abortion takes place. Even if the two are not close, it can be upsetting to the father to be left in the dark and find out later.

Actually, the best way to have control over one's body, if you are a woman, is to not allow yourself to get pregnant in the first place (if you don't want to be). Use birth control, or have surgery that prevents you from being impregnated (or perhaps, if you are married, your husband could have a vasectomy instead of you having your tubes tied). You can also abstain from sex until birth control is a sure thing (during certain times of the month). Want the baby, if you know you could get pregnant. Be generally able to take care of the baby, if you know you could get pregnant. Don't be careless and foolish about sex and well realize the outcomes that come from having sex. A potential baby's needs and care should have priority over your desire for sexual gratification. Consider that. The baby will be part of you. A baby can live and grow to adulthood and end out living eighty years, or even longer. Someone is going to have to take care of that baby and take care of it, well, until the baby is the age of majority. An abortion will end the baby's life; the baby will be 'no more'. The sex act can take place in just a couple of minutes. If you are young and are having sex, do you get the picture? Do you really get it?

Healthy sexuality exists when two people are mutually satisfied and have positive firm feelings that what they are doing is right before their God. In America, most people who believe in God are Christians, but, obviously, not all are. America is still a Christian nation. Many are Catholic. There is freedom of religion in America so people can believe differently from other people. How others react to a couple's relationship or their life together is somewhat inconsequential if the couple is God-focused because God-focused people believe that if you go God's way, He will be with you. Those who make a covenant with God and decide to stick to it can also make a covenant in a marriage and decide to stick to that. They will have greater solidarity. That is logical, when you think about it. Having a good marriage is the ideal, and it is not so easy to achieve or attain what is ideal because what is ideal can be illusive. Even when there is effort, there can still be problems and woes.

Again, the umbrella of a successful marriage is commitment. A commitment is a type of covenant. It's a bond you should not break. Many believe that what you do in life, and what you don't do, will meet with judgment, and that God has established how people should live. You find this in all the religions. With reference to Christianity and the views of Christians, it is believed that everything that is in the Bible is what people should live by. All questions are answered when a person knows the Bible. The Bible never fails to answer a question it itself may raise. God has put in the Bible, by way of divinely-inspired people, everything He wanted for people to know, as a basis for living. The Bible is complete and discoverable and two people who take Christian living seriously can have a successful marriage by trusting in God to supply their needs and by committing to prayer their burdens, fears, and concerns. Many people live by these precepts, and the spiritual dimension is strong in these people's lives.

Other Faiths live by other books and teachings, and they essentially believe the same principles. Other Faiths have a different holy book they follow. I'm touching on Christianity because America is essentially a Christian nation, relative to its overall population. Per capita, America is more Christian than anything else. Still, there is diversity, and people accept and even embrace diversity. Many believe there are a number of paths to God.

Christians also believe that men should take the lead for spiritual growth of a couple. For example, men should round up the family for church services and encourage their church involvement. Many Christian men do not assume this leadership, though, and these kinds of tasks fall on the woman. For Christians, it's also thought that men should lead the family in prayer, and in Bible study from time to time. Not that many men actually do this. Women tend to start up these kinds of family-oriented talks more often than men do. Sharing such tasks can be good, though, but these days, Christian women tend to be pretty strong. Women make good leaders, actually, but in a Christian marriage, men are supposed to be the head of the home. Too many men fall short of doing this—of knowing how to do this, and of being able to do this. Some Christian men do not even know about this perspective. Resolve can jumpstart anything, though.

Other religions put man at the head of the home, too. Quite a few do, and so many wonder 'is that really God-ordained'? Some men will abuse this position, and look at it all wrong. They will act like they are more important than the woman, and they aren't. The woman is always of equal importance, and frankly, some women are more the head of the home because the man puts in little effort and doesn't know how to be head of the home. He doesn't care to find out how to, either. Still and all, marriage is a joint effort requiring give and take. Women are equal as to input and importance. It has to be added that many couples do not go the way of religion when it comes to marriage, and they are happy and thriving.

Many men need to get rid of negative things in their life if what is negative is holding them back from being able to be head of their home and if that is what they want to do. Some men need to be better trained before they can even be leaders of themselves, let alone be leaders of others. This is not to imply that some men aren't good leaders, because we all know that many certainly are and they deserve their position. Some men are wise and fair and moral. But others need to find some help for themselves so they can improve as human beings. Then, they can perhaps manage a home better. Growth and improvement is what it's all about. Counseling could be of benefit to them, but they might need to 'shop counselors' and arrange their own counseling schedule. Some men will seek help from a minister.

# Chapter 9

## The Benefits of Counseling

Strong, faith-based homes—whatever the religion—will help keep America strong. Any strong home will, actually. Individuals can progress faster and society can be maintained when home and family is being sustained and preserved. Children in faith-based homes tend to mature faster (in ways that some consider important). Spouses who live by a strong faith contribute more positively to the stabilization of a community, and to the individuals whose lives they touch. Sex is important in a marriage no matter how old the people are because the intimacy and the enjoyment of sex help to keep the marriage alive and the two people together. Most people believe that sex should have a spiritual dimension to it and that the spiritual dimension elevates everything.

The spiritual dimension of a marriage should not be ignored. It should be given priority. Of course 'spiritual' means different things to different people. Some people may think one idea is spiritual, whereas other people may think that the same idea was just an idea, like every other idea is an idea. Spiritual receptivity and interpretations vary immensely among people. Still, having a generally-shared spiritual perspective can generally help bond two people and keep them together.

People need to see good families functioning in society so they will be drawn in to want this for themselves. The family is important to society and so are marriages, obviously, because for one thing, marriages are what produce families. Without families, society would be splintered and weak. Countries would take over other countries. There would be less to fight for, especially if there weren't many children needing protecting. The family is needed to sustain the individuals within it. Society profits from happy rather than unhappy homes. Children are hurt when they are around unhappy or extremely troubled homes. Children become what they see. They grow up with baggage, which can be heavy to carry into their own, separate lives. Some will create the baggage for themselves, though. Their baggage may have nothing to do with their parents. If you ever watch the TV show, *Baggage*, which tries to pair people up, you'll quickly realize that accumulated baggage generally relates to free-will choices that have been made on the part of these, generally, under-30s people.

To emphasize, a marriage does not have to be Christian to be successful. Many people live their lives within perspectives that differ from Christianity, or, they might be non-serious Christians who believe in the Bible but they don't necessarily practice Christianity in a strict way, or even much at all. Many such people can have successful marriages. Successful marriages can be found anywhere, and within different Faiths. Certain positives in marriages, like sexual enjoyment, commitment, hard work, respect, loyalty, affection, and even friendship have kept marriages together and they will continue to do so for as long as society remains generally stable and the economy stays relatively strong, or stays strong enough.

Sex doesn't have to be perfect in a marriage but it does need to be there or something will definitely be missing from the marriage. Sex gives people something to look forward to. Because of sex, people work harder at their marriage. Sex is an incentive. Humanity is dependent on sex, but sexual desire must be channeled right and expressed in loving ways or society will decay. The word, decadent, relates to the word, decay. Human sexuality must be placed in the right and proper perspective or there will be chaos. Living in and around chaos brings about stress, discord, and unhappiness.

Often, people have to put up with a great deal in a marriage, especially at certain times, but if the two people decide, early on, that they are in the marriage for keeps, they'll put more effort and heart into working out their problems. They will understand the need to occasionally compromise and will be accepting of that and will realize that they will have to live with compromise, from time to time. People who decide to have and to keep a good sex life will be amazed at how good their marriage will stay. It is not good to let that part of a marriage fall by the wayside. Too many people do, and they're just not as happy as they could be.

If one person in the marriage is noticeably arrogant, stubborn, and selfish, usually sex will decrease and it can even become non-existent in a marriage. Such a situation can happen suddenly or it can occur over a period of time and any similar behavior can weaken a marriage rather quickly. Divorce may eventually result. The key is, do not allow yourself to be arrogant, stubborn, and selfish. You will lose the genuine affection and respect of others if you do, which includes affection and respect in the bedroom, with your spouse. When there are any negative behaviors in a marriage, somebody in the marriage or both individuals should consider seeking a counselor.

Counselors and professionals need to advise their clients of many things, or help their clients to arrive at conclusions on their own. Counselors need to have their own perspective about marriage and sexuality sharpened, like a pencil is sharpened and prepared for use. People should seek out counselors that seem to have it all together in that they live and work within structure, clarity, and assurance. If a counselor does not seem to be compassionate and understanding, possibly find another counselor. But, you don't want a counselor that coddles and is too agreeable about too many things because you want a straight shooter. A counselor should still try to be objective when they are with clients. I know this seems inconsistent, but it really isn't. A counselor can have a personal foundation that results in having a personal consistency, and they can still be objective and keep most all of their views to themselves. If a selected counselor doesn't seem to be generally objective, maybe find a different counselor.

A counselor should know what their own beliefs and values are so they will not go in an aimless direction. Even other counselors agree that a counselor should stay objective. Counselors should not try to impose their values on others, especially if individuals are resistant to their approach or orientation. Imposing never works. Present things, when and as it seems fitting to do so, but don't impose. People have to make up their own mind and make their own decisions. People want to make their own decisions. If a counselor is objective yet still holds to a personal value system, they won't be wishy-washy and inconsistent just because their various clients believe different things. This is the point so look for a steadfast and unimposing counselor that stays within a general foundation and doesn't go all over the place.

You want to get to know your counselor and know a few things about your counselor. A counselor should always hope that they will make a difference, and they might, but they shouldn't count on that because people have minds of their own. If a selected counselor seems to get too wrapped up in their clients, consider finding a counselor that is more aloof and detached. You do not want a counselor to be your friend—on your side, yes and up to a point, but not your friend. No client should get too attached to a counselor and vice versa because the relationship has to be and stay a more formal one. People have to work through things after they leave a counselor's office and counselors can't be with them then. You want a counselor who interjects occasional thoughts and ideas in a general manner so there can be food for thought as you go along and after you leave. You don't want a counselor that seems like a stone. (Some counselors can be like that.) Hopefully, some of the counselor's directives will stick and be helpful, in the short run and/or the long run. A counselor ploughs through and does their best. That is all they can do. Try to find a counselor who seems to care and is genuinely trying to help. Look for sincerity.

A counselor can never expect too much as counseling sessions go along, though, because the mind is complex. Most counselors lean on the belief that they are doing some good but that the good they are doing, in general, cannot be measured. Even when any good seems to be present, a counselor will still, technically, not be able to measure the progress. If there are positive and apparent results, a counselor can say "well, there appears to be progress" or "presently, I suspect there's been progress", but that's as far as a counselor can go because no counselor knows the future and no counselor can know all the intricacies of a person's mind at any given time. Generally, there is always 'some' progress, though, so counselors can be happy with that. That is obviously logical but to know how much progress there's been and to measure the progress—that can be illusive, particularly early on. This is one reason I established the Gap Theory as a new counseling approach. Progress can be measured.

Again, the Gap Theory has been introduced and explained in my book, *Crime and Rehabilitation*. Even the gaps are listed and there are fifty-seven of them but new ones could be added—not too many, though. The actual listed gaps get filled in as time goes by (this achievement can become clear and evident in certain areas along the way). With the Gap Theory (as opposed to using and applying other Psychological or Counseling Theories,) progress can not only be noted but it can specifically be noted. This is because specific gaps are listed. A client can figure out if and when a gap gets filled in. So can the counselor. The Gap Theory could be used for pre-marital counseling, easily. It could be used for most any kind of counseling. I've also written a short booklet on just the Gap Theory, under that title. It is the same content that is worked into the *Crime and Rehabilitation* book.

If people who want to get married go in for pre-marital counseling, they should go in for the counseling for a number of sessions and they should be honest with themselves during any of the counseling sessions. If they're not ready for marriage, they're not. A wedding can always be deferred or even cancelled. Who to marry and when to marry are two of the most important decisions anyone will ever make. As noted earlier, the TV series, *Married at First Sight* (2014-2019), featured real but sight-unseen weddings (and marriages). Four couples got married on the show, for each series. A group of professional experts on the show put the couples together based on what they believed to be compatibility factors. (They do not meet each other before the marriage; on one level, it is really a temporary marriage because they know they can divorce at the end, if they want to.)

Observing the interactions and the dynamics of the different couples is what was fascinating (in that they were actually just married and were new to living as marrieds). They went on a honeymoon, moved in together, lived together for a while, and then decided if they wanted to stay together or split up and get a divorce. (The production would pay for any divorces.) The camera followed the couples around. The camera was as a voyeur.

The professional experts were on the show, periodically, providing counseling to the couples, and giving commentary and views, which gave the series more stability and authenticity. Two couples ended out staying together at the end of the one particular series I watched; two did, with the other series I watched, but then soon after, both of those relationships ended. One ended a little harshly; the other one, very amicably. In fact, with the amicable one, the couple seemed to get back together later on, but it was hard to tell if they had or hadn't. Another series after those two didn't have much pairing at the end, except for one couple, but they split up afterwards. With yet another series, two couples seemed to get along all-right, but one couple was filled with passion whereas the other couple was platonic (for some time). Another couple fought because she was not a smoker and he had put down on the application that he smoked occasionally when he secretly had a chain-smoking habit and she kept smelling tobacco smoke on him. She did not like being around smoke. (Some Internet after-commenters believed it could be marijuana smoking he was engaging in, which at the time was illegal.) He became defensive with her and argumentative and turned around and tried to find fault with her, which appeared to be a disrespectful, unfair modus operandi and it alienated the woman even further. (This kind of behavior occurs when someone does not want to get rid of a habit.) He made it impossible for her to trust him, and to, therefore, stay in. You pretty much knew that in the end and even if they had made it some distance, they wouldn't end out staying together.

The disappointed woman got flak from the spouse, not co-operation, on a matter that had been important to her (i.e. not smoking). He was too reactive and defensive, too fast. She was quite a steady person. She took it all in stride. He also ended out giving his wedding ring to a perfect stranger (on film and just for show), just because he wanted to be rid of it, as a closure gesture. The two broke off early in the show—no surprise. Two other couples (both mixed couples—Anglo and Hispanic) stayed together at the end of the show and all four seemed happy. They were all rooted in Florida.

Then, one of the series came along later that feature two black couples and two white couples and that one was really gripping. It was filmed in several cities. Professional people (in this overall field) have loved this marriage-related show. At the start, two couples seemed to be going along just fine and two weren't. With the two that weren't, it related to lack of physical attraction. One tied in with communication problems. So far so good on some of the show's relationships and so, since a few couples stayed married, how soon would it be before the children would start coming is what viewers were wondering. If you are thinking about getting married, try to watch shows like this one. If you are already married, try to watch shows like this one. You will learn a lot. Watch any marriage-related shows.

A couple of other interesting shows about marriage that came down the pike centered on wedding planning—*My Fair Wedding* (2008) and *My Great Big Live Wedding* (2018). A professional wedding planner named David Tutera somehow comes across two people who are planning to be married and he organizes amazing weddings for them in both these shows. In the second-noted one, there is usually something sympathetic relating to one or both of the people who are to be married and you get to know them and learn about their story before and as they are in process of getting married.

In marriage, it is important to be co-operative and even conciliatory with the marital partner, in a genuine way, or there can be little happiness. Love, instead of growing, can actually die. Both people have to be givers to the relationship on a consistent basis. It doesn't work well if only one person is a giver. The non-giver will eventually lose out, and he or she will cause excess stress and some unhappiness in the meantime. Marriage is serious business. You have to be a giver. Both must keep on giving, but giving should be naturally and mutually done. Both have to want to give.

The problem with the married-at-first sight method of marrying (sight unseen) is that there can be no steady courtship. In the noted TV series, each partner had not even met the other partner before they were married (in a real marriage ceremony with white dress/tuxedo, friends and family, minister, and the 'I do-s'). The marriages in each series were essentially arranged, but the couples could decide, at the end of the eight weeks, if they wanted to stay together or get a divorce, which they chose to do while they were on air. Again, the divorce was at no cost to them if that is what they were going to decide to do.

During the eight weeks, as the show went along, they certainly got to know each other, but it was after the fact. Again, there was never any courtship prior to the marriage so the individuals who got married had no way of getting to know their partner, in advance. Free-will choice was out the window, in other words. The couples usually tended to wait a while to get to know the other person before they consummated the marriage (more seemed to wait for a while, than didn't) so sex was put on hold (until the couple was comfortable with it). But, it didn't have to be put on hold because they were now formally and legally married. In real life situations, though, and with many people, there is sex before marriage and that can cause problems and be too much too fast because the two didn't get to know the other person well enough before they became intimate. Some are able to handle this and others aren't.

As noted before, there is a television series titled *90 Day Fiancé* (2014 to 2021) and the couples were obviously not yet married. In this reality show, one person in the couple is from another country other than America, and the other person is from America. Another television presentation that came around was *Why Did I Get Married?* (2007). These were a series of reality shows that featured couples who went to a reunion at the same time and ended out having to deal with various marital issues.

Again, for couples about to be married or couples currently married, these shows can be enlightening, whether they're watched separately or together, as a couple. (Many households have two television sets so some programs are not watched together.) Some really should be watched together, though, and these kinds of shows are good examples of what should, perhaps, be watched together.

Another show, that's been around for a long time, is *The Newlywed Game*. It evolved and it eventually had to be on late-night because it became more sex-focused in rather direct ways. At first it was on around the time range of prime time so it was on early evening, when families were watching. Originally, sex-type questions on the show were mild and ambiguous or cryptic. There were very few of them. Couples were more embarrassed about their personal sex life back then, and they would act embarrassed if questions got personal. On the later one that was on late night, some of the questions on the show got to be extremely personal about sex but late night draws in a different audience. The kids are supposed to be asleep.

If you are soon to be married, or are married, there can be benefits to watching some of these shows, but always keep to what you know is your own perspective when you watch these shows if you <u>know</u> it is the perspective you wish to hold to. Don't let yourself get carried away with what other marrieds are thinking or doing. Know what you, alone, believe and think. Still, you can pick up some good pointers, especially about relationships, when watching these shows.

The idea of intelligently-arranged marriages is food for thought (like what is shown on *Married at First Sight*). In certain countries around the world, many marriages are formally arranged, usually by the parents of the bride and the groom. It is not a trial marriage. There is no option to divorce after a given time. These young people may know each other fairly well, or not at all. Some of these marriages work out all-right. There are close ties with parents and they don't want to disappoint their parents. There used to be more of these arranged marriages, per capita, but they are still around. You find this in many societies.

Today, there are Internet dating sites and people can meet people who they're interested in, that way. You find out details about someone you might date and then meet them, somewhat sight unseen. There are pictures, though, and sometimes videos. Friends can be made this way, too. Marriage is always possible by way of these dating sites. There are quite a few of these sites on-line now. A person can even try several of them. Daters must be careful, though. There can be misrepresentations on-line, and even some dangerous people.

If you are older and you have kids who are about to get married, consider offering to pay for their pre-marital counseling, as a gift. They may not have even thought about going in for counseling. It would probably be better to do this than to buy the young people some dishes or stainless flatware. They likely don't have much money for counseling, themselves, if they're just starting out. Grandparents can offer to pay for some or all of this counseling, too. Think of what a good investment pre-marital counseling would be, prior to a marriage. A number of young people, and even older people, will seek counseling through their church, synagogue, temple, or mosque, prior to getting married. Find a good counselor, though, if any counseling is to take place apart from a church, synagogue, temple, or mosque. Double dip. Get counseling at a church, synagogue, temple, or mosque <u>and</u> at a counselor's office. People should really be looking for red flags, even up to the marriage ceremony.

Anyone already in a marriage should consider going in for counseling, at least every so often. Even if you go in one time every month of the year, that would be better than never going in. It's always best to go in a few times in a row, though, at least at the start. Quite a few people go in for counseling just once a month. Some people go in twice a month. Some will go in if an emergency comes up. Even just once every three months might be all right, for some. When you go in for counseling, you are caring about the marriage and focusing in on the marriage. Marriage takes steady work. If there are mounting problems in the marriage and if you can afford to go in fairly regularly for counseling, your marriage might be saved and your life will probably be better. Some people will go in for counseling only at different times during their life. It can be very random. Counseling is around, for people who are interested. Some things can hit a marriage and be overwhelming. When that happens, call and make an immediate appointment.

There are many different problems that can hit a marriage. They are diverse. Some of them can be really petty but they can still weigh heavily on one or both partner's minds. Some marriages can have some really big and significant problems and outside people will wonder how the couple will ever get through them. Such stress situations can put a burden on a counselor, quite frankly. It's extra strain when a client of theirs has severe problems. Frankly, some people cannot 'communicate' their way out of their problems, not per se. Communication will help, but there are other ways their problems may have to be tackled. Usually, work and effort will be needed but both may only be part of the solution. So many times, money troubles and money management are at the root. There can be medical problems, too.

Infidelity is another reason why people need counseling. In the mid-2010s, it was uncovered that there are social-related websites where people can go to seek out someone they can have an extra-marital affair with. The sites are similar to a dating site, only the participants are married. Names on one site (the Ashley Madison site) were hacked. On the list, 90,000 enrolled names were entered but 20,000 had actually paid for the services and had gone past the point of being a near-participant or mere onlooker. The revelation of the website (and certain of the names) was shocking to many. Several divorces were filed—by wives, mainly—after the revelations. Just the mere contacting of these kinds of websites points to the breaking of marriage vows since <u>intent</u> to cheat is the beginning of the cheating and is essentially cheating. Quite a few of these people found someone (or several) to cheat on their partner with—many did, more than once. There were even some suicides after the uncovering (and the posting of names) because men were humiliated, frankly, and it was men who used that site (for the most part).

All in all, around 33 million men had <u>visited</u> the site (versus only around 3 million women). No one knows for sure, of the ones who actually enrolled and paid for the service, followed through with the adultery but once there was a payment, you would assume all of them did. Affected women (wives) were both hurt and angry. And, what about STDs? The men would have just gone on like nothing had happened, had they not been exposed. The company was sued because of the leaks. Some people on the list were blackmailed by outside people who claimed they would report the exposure to wives and families. People from other countries were also on the list. Again, there are several smaller companies and Internet sites of this ilk. Will they, too, be hacked and will participants be exposed? Hacking of Internet data seems to be fair game these days, so nothing is ever really a hundred percent safe and secret.

Counselors are used to dealing with infidelity. Many different types of problems come their way. They can get some very unusual problems, but all will be confidential. There are good conscientious counselors out there. Counselors want to help. They're trained to want to do that so don't allow yourself to be cynical of counselors, as some people allow themselves to be. Give a trained professional a chance. Counselors have a unique and individual type of Education, assuming they completed a counseling program at an accredited college. They completed a good deal of coursework, of a variety, and a Practicum, and a Comprehensive test. Plus, they usually have some experience. They experienced 'life in a classroom' and then some. Many trained counselors live and breathe counseling. They have a preparation that relates to counseling and that others do not have. Anyone can hang up a shingle and say they are a counselor, but what, really, has been their preparation background?

Many people consider counseling to be a necessity. Some consider it to be a luxury. If you don't give it a try, you can't possibly know what you're missing. Many people acknowledge that they have benefited greatly from counseling. They're happy about their growth, and with some outcomes. Frankly, it is usually the more neurotic or less integrated people who fight the idea of counseling. No matter who you are or how old you are, counseling will improve your life if you find a good counselor. Again, consider trying more than one out. Just go fishing.

Counseling is one avenue to go down, for self-improvement. It is always a benefit to establish a one-on-one relationship with a person who has special training and who wants to help you. You don't want an overly friendly and overly permissive and accepting counselor. You want a counselor to be, and stay generally objective, regardless of the approach they might take. You want a counselor who is at least cordial, but who is also somewhat aloof and even, at times, distant. After all, you are the one who is supposed to be processing. You can also seek out a psychologist or even a psychiatrist. Both are qualified to counsel people. A psychologist will have taken different classes than a counselor has taken. Some counselors have a Master's Degree. Some psychologists will get a PhD. Psychiatrists have a medical degree. They are all counselors because they counsel people with the intent to help them.

People who are having some kind of sexual or sexuality problem can go in for counseling for a specific problem, but actually, if they went in for general counseling, often their specific sex-related problem can be solved or worked through because it may relate to something more general that gets discussed during general counseling. The specific problem may not even need to be openly discussed, per se. What comes out of the counseling session may be general but the client can make a connection from what is general to what is specific. General counseling can bring about growth and awareness and growth and awareness can end out having many applications and be quite helpful.

The overall field of sex was given scope in the United States by Alfred C. Kinsey, who was a Zoology professor at Indiana University at Bloomington, Indiana, years ago. Much of his work was done in the 1940s and 1950s. He is very famous. He began doing interviews on the side with some of his students when he was teaching a class that covered aspects of sexual reproduction and sex, in general, including the subjects of technique, physiology, and contraception. As time went by, he collected numerous sex histories of various students. There was very little promiscuity going on at the time. Gradually, he compiled statistical data from the accumulation of answered questions, and he got the data from one or more questionnaires that he used.

Kinsey left the field of Zoology, and his study of insects to do human sexuality studies, of adults. He had published work on the Gall Wasp and it had emphasized that each wasp acted and behaved differently from the other wasps. He was somehow able to use that conclusion as a basis for his studies on sex, which must have been interesting, in itself. How captured wasps could effectively be observed is anyone's guess, and do wasps really behave all that differently out in the wild? Watching wasps all day could not have been easy so you can understand why he jumped at the chance to research human sexual behavior. It would have been so much more interesting.

One Kinsey Report came out in 1948 and it was titled, *The Sexual Behavior in the Human Male*. The Rockefeller Association had awarded him money to interview individuals about their sex histories (these interviewees were no longer the college students). Kinsey was to compile all the related data. Kinsey was now able to work with mainstream people, versus the college students he had been working with, before. Basically, though, he was now compiling information and drawing some simple and obvious conclusions based on his compilations. People tended to disagree with many of his conclusions—his statistics, included. His research tended to anger many, in fact—but the Rockefeller Association continued to finance him for several more years. With Kinsey's reports, too, you really have to see the questionnaires before you can accept his compilations and conclusions. You have to see how the questions are all worded or you will misconstrue everything, including any of his results. It is always all in the wording.

Sex research is very hard to compile and can be slanted and biased. Reading these kinds of reports can be helpful for married couples but there is much more to them than what is surface. There have been more studies and reports or findings that relate to different aspects of sex since Kinsey's work was done. Some are considerably more recent than those of Kinsey. There are books out on these studies, and there are plenty of books out about sex, too—lots of them. The books I'm referring to are not at all pornographic; they're educational and can be enlightening and helpful to anyone but you have to be very discerning when you read them.

Masters and Johnson did research and came out with some reports from their studies, too, which were done from around 1957 to 1965. Some couples wanted to participate in the study and in doing the sex research. It was noted that the participating helped the participant's sex lives—both directly and indirectly. Masters and Johnson studied around 380 women and 310 men on the subject of sexual response. They also did conversion studies, and some work relative to homosexuals, claiming to have about a six-year 70% success rate (i.e. the homosexuals turned back to being heterosexuals). At the time, the American Psychiatric Association had classified homosexuality as a psychological and sexual disorder and this is why Masters and Johnson had attempted conversion. However, the homosexual classification was repealed soon afterwards.

With Kinsey's studies, these mainstream people were paid for their time, as were Kinsey and his three associates. The researchers were able to get the people to open up about their sex lives because the pitch was—it was all for scientific research and education. They kept getting support from the Rockefeller Association and they kept compiling information about both females and males. Three hundred questions were asked of each person and, as time went by, more and more people were questioned—way too many were, some say. Some were not at all happy with the taboo subjects that he researched and covered. Some think the study was too long and that it involved too many people.

Supposedly, Kinsey himself began practicing some out-of-the-range-of-normalcy sex behavior and practices, assumedly for the sake of his research and study. He also encouraged his three associates to do the same. There were different views about homosexuals back then. There may have been some wife swapping, homosexuality, et al. (with his workers and doing what was experimental). Wife swapping was literally and absolutely unheard of in main society because it was essentially non-existent, and for the most part, so was homosexuality. What little homosexuality there was, was underground because it was so opposed to by essentially all of society. You never read about it in books. You never heard about it (but were appalled if you did). You never knew anyone, or of anyone, who was. Homosexuality was a criminal offense in some areas.

The way some people today indicate, homosexuality was all over the place but that is not true. Very few cases of homosexuality were even around—almost none were. Facts have even been made up about that. Any facts there may have been about such issues were played down, not exaggerated during those times. Today, it all gets played up when people really only want true facts. Of course, yesterday was yesterday and today is today. Everything has changed. In the mid-1950s, the Rockefeller Association pulled the plug on Kinsey's research and studies, but by then, *The Sexual Behavior in the Human Female* had already been published, in 1953. There is still a Rockefeller Foundation. It has lasted a long time. It is different from the one back set up back in the 1950s.

Kinsey believed there was too much sexual repression because of the previous Victorian Age, because of prudish ideas in the home, because of psychological disorders that led to frigidity and guilt about sex, and even because of an increase in venereal diseases (but they were really very low in incidence and number, at the time). Syphilis was minimally around. It had somewhat been around for a long time even before then. In the 1940s and 1950s, only sex within marriage was acceptable in society. Unwanted pregnancies were feared if a couple was not married, because of the stigma that was attached. Therefore, there was little pre-marital sex, and lots of general, out-in-the-public courtship. There was no birth control, and women couldn't run out and get an abortion.

Back then, men actually preferred marrying virgins (and most women were). Slight necking was all right, but not petting. (You don't hear those two words much, anymore, because so many young people go past that.) Homosexuality was rare—very—but there were a few gay men around for Kinsey to be able to do some research and study the subject. The word, gay, was not being used back then—only 'homosexual' was. (So was the word, queer, which is an outdated word.) People today like to think there were many gays around back then, but no, most men chose heterosexuality (and certainly, so, too, with women) or they just kept to themselves and lived a solitary life. That was the societal norm. There was no choice in the matter—you went 'mainstream'. You wanted to fit in and conform. Christianity was quite entrenched. Many people had Bibles and went to church.

The culture and societal norms and values were so different then and so Kinsey's research and studies have less value today than they did during Kinsey's day. At the time and for some time, many people scoffed at his work. They didn't take it seriously. In some ways, though, he was ahead of his time. Today, he has somewhat been forgotten. Any book on Kinsey, or film or documentary done about him, is not apt to be completely accurate. It is <u>old</u> books and writings about him that tell his story. They are a little hard to find. Most of them are out of print.

Kinsey went in to interview closet gays. They were found in very few bars in the larger cities of America. These weren't all-gay bars, just general bars. Gay men were few and were very hard to find but he found a few and compiled data about their sex lives. Back then, it was termed the homosexual underworld. He found almost no lesbians in the 1940s and 1950s. He died in 1956 of a heart attack, at age 62. He did studies on the darker aspects of sexuality, as well—masochism being one of the subjects. Kinsey was able to find one known pedophile. He really didn't learn much about that unorthodox practice, with such a limited sampling (of only the one man). Many crimes, back then, genuinely were not around, and there were genuinely so few gays (contrary to what you sometimes hear or see in films, today).

Kinsey formalized his studies and findings and they were academically done, but there has still been criticism about his body of work. The Rockefeller Association had felt that a four hundred- person sample was population enough for such research or study. Kinsey went beyond that anyway, and was able to keep getting money from the Rockefeller Association, at least for a time. Kinsey had even filmed sexual acts; some were, perhaps, of his Associates. In short, there was nothing he wouldn't do to get information for his studies and to explore the full range of sexuality. Some information and statistics weren't available to him, though, because of too limited of a sampling. Life was morally different then, despite what you see in today's movies and even documentaries. It wasn't, so much, different because of sexual repression because most people married fairly young, and also, people wanted to be sexually pure because it was the norm. People weren't really even thinking of being repressed.

People today can read his reports and learn what they can about his findings. A lot of it is in archives, though. Some of what he acquired might have had some validity, but we really can't know that for sure because we weren't there? From around 1970 on, there has been a sexual revolution, not only in the United States, but in other countries around the world, too. This revolution or push for sexual freedom had more to do with an influx of illegal drugs than it did with the Kinsey compilations or with any other sex studies. (The arrival of birth-control pills played a part, too.)

Illegal drugs and pushing sexual boundaries seemed to go together, and it started not so much with the Beatniks, but with the Hippies and Flower Children, and the Viet Nam War because that is when drugs started to flood in. True, drugs had always been around, some, and they had been here and there, somewhat, but a lot of drugs came in from foreign countries during the 1970s. Some were manufactured nearby. There were amphetamines (speed) and LSD, and there was lots of hemp and marijuana. Before the 1970s, the average person never even saw drugs or knew anyone who was using any.

The studies Kinsey did essentially excluded minorities. Again, it was difficult if not impossible during Kinsey's time to find enough people who were a part of the sexually marginalized group (versus the mainstream group). Many people did not want to even participate in his studies. Things were so sacred and private back then. Few wanted to have their sex life—thoughts and patterns—exposed and they only did it for the money they were paid, as participants. Today, there would be plenty of volunteers for these kinds of studies, but is there a need for them? Most people these days are quite sexually aware.

Counselors and psychologists are supposed to keep up with sex research findings so they can be better at their job. Anyone who is married and interested in the subject can ask a counselor about past or recent research. They're supposed to know, at least generally. Research results may not always relate to today's married couples, or to specific married couples, either. Like-samplings are what are needed so findings can be more reliable and adaptable.

Sex makes the world go around. It is going on all around us, all the time. Too many people make jokes about sex and some jokes are off-color, or they're really sick. Sex is not a laughing matter. Some comedians dirtify sex. Some and certain jokes about sex are all-right but many are not. Certain jokes distort the meaning of sex—that is the point. Sex is really a private matter. It is what it is—a part of life and that which people want and need. It can be beautiful, if it occurs in the right context and with the right person.

Again, there are weird, sick people in this world and this gets into crime. Sexual deviants have to want to get help. They have to want to help themselves, so they can change. (A few cannot be helped—not much, anyway.) The counseling that a regular citizen might receive for their problem or problems is not going to be the same as the counseling a sexual deviant would receive for their problem or problems. You cannot lump all counseling into the same bowl because people are all so different. The same counseling approach cannot be used for all people. There are some approaches that tend to work for the mainstream, however.

If obtaining counseling is a person's genuine goal and they follow through with it, that person will end out seeing a much bigger picture. To emphasis, everyone should leave their reserve behind and go in for counseling, at least every so often. Some counselors will give you one half-hour of no-charge counseling. Always ask about that, and also about any discounts, should you be eligible for any.

Counseling can alter or change someone's attitude and perspective. It can help to clarify muddled thinking. Counseling can rescue people—from dilemmas and situations. It can help show people the way through dilemmas and situations. Counseling can help to decrease or eliminate oppression and frustration. Gaining insight will come with the counseling. Counseling can help people figure out what it is that they need to do, so counseling can be directive. Counseling can be constructive for those who choose to seek it. Couples can go in together, or each person can go in separately. Or, the couple can go in together at times, and each person can go in separately at other times. They can go in for just a little counseling, or for a lot of counseling. To emphasize, some counseling is certainly better than none, and getting a start with counseling is better than doing nothing. At least you will be making an effort to take charge.

If sex is to be good in a relationship and willing reciprocity is to stay present with each partner, there has to be an equality that is clear and evident, relative to the two people. It cannot be feigned, artificial, or pretended. The equality must have validity. On *The View*, in October of 2016, Vice Presidential candidate Tim Kaine and his wife were on one of the segments. It was more than obvious (no one could miss it) how equal both partners were in their marriage. He lifted his wife up more than once, and complimented her. She essentially did the same but he did this a little more than she did. <u>By example</u>, he showed the viewers the authentic and existing equality that has been present in their relationship. It stood out.

There should be equality in a marriage. It is a necessary perception and the partners should be aware of this equality. In some Middle-East cultures, there is no equality and men control and dominate not only their wife (or wives, in some cases), but all women. Women are stifled, thwarted, and opposed at many bends and turns. Women risk being beaten and even killed. Some women must wear a ridiculous and cumbersome outer garment that is ugly and that hides their face (burkas, et al.). Some wear a hijab, which is not like a burka. It is a head covering, in the main. (A scarf or head covering is not so bad and you would think that would be enough—that, and generally modest clothing.) The outer garment (i.e. the burka and similar outer wear) is heavy and cumbersome. God forbid if any flesh were to show, were women to wear something different. Some women can't even have their face showing.

Women trip on these long, heavy garments, and they sweat profusely under them when their body reaches a certain temperature. Air does not get in to the body area, like a light-weight full dress would (especially a cotton one). Even if the material used were to be thinner, no air would get to body areas because the whole body has to be covered down to the shoes. They generally don't use material that breathes. Material is usually heavy so it falls down tighter on the body. It can be torturous for women to wear these garments. Their men ought to try wearing them . . . so they'll know and allow in change. The over-heating restricts their movement. These outer garments are black so they absorb heat. When the face is hidden, their vision is obstructed, like when a mask or a visor or screen will obstruct someone's vision. You can't get much work done when you wear these long outer garments and these face coverings.

In some places, an abaya is worn along with a hijab. An abaya is like a burka because it is a full-length covering or dressing that covers all of the body. It can be lighter in weight than the burkas, however. Colors of abayas can be varied but not too strong. If you are a woman, you cannot draw attention to yourself in any way. With the hijab, no hair can show. It covers the head completely. It is not like a scarf that is usually less covering and open at the bottom. Only the face shows with the hijab. You cannot wear make-up, either, so your face will look better. God forbid if you should look attractive and look good for observing men.

The countries that force the wearing of such inconvenient garments on women are male-dominated countries, to the extreme. Women can't even go out in public without a male escort. They aren't allowed to drive on their own. An 'escorting' male has to drive them. Women in these stifling and smothering societies have to be very careful about what they say, and what they do. They are dominated in their home, and by their government. Some women in these countries are forced into polygamy. The male marries several or many females. Some individuals in the Mormon Faith practice polygamy. More of them might like to but it's against the law, in many places.

Polygamy was in the Old Testament, but it was small-scale. Some believe that God allowed it so the population would increase faster. The world was not populated to any great degree during Old Testament times. Men died in battle, too. Many groups were at-odds with the Jewish Faith and forced them into various battles. A number of men died. There was, then, a shortage of men. With more women than men, after one or more battles, women needed husbands, and babies needed to be born. Now, population growth is fast. It has been considerable and even excessive.

In many areas, there's been too much population growth—hence all the pollution, greenhouse gasses, and bad $CO_2$ layers, here and there and ever on the increase. (My book *Global Warming Causes, Solutions, and Theories* covers this subject and so much more.) We certainly don't need polygamy to run rampant anywhere because we need to slow down population increase. Some people should perhaps, even, volunteer to only have one child. Perhaps all people should? (Note I use the word, volunteer.) The New Testament dispelled polygamy, and within it are a number of marriage laws. Old Testament History is long past. Today is what matters.

Women's rights are scoffed at by men who hold to such choking views. Some men purposely want to restrict many freedoms. Women are their property and they give them no free rein, whatsoever. How would these men like to wear these garments and face covers? Why don't they? It's all right for women to wear them, but not the men? Men there believe they are too good to have to wear them. If women choose to be covered, let them at least wear something lighter-weighing, more open to the air, and more comfortable. Why can't they show at least some skin? What is wrong with arms and legs showing? Why do they have to hide their head and face? And their whole body?

A few Middle-East countries will encourage some women's freedoms, however. Some allow more than others allow and it is all relative. There are eighteen Middle-East countries. The countries that depend on democratized countries seem to give women the most space. Since the computer and the Internet entered the scene, more people see women as being valuable assets to a country. Home life has improved for many women around the world because of the Internet. Some Western ideas have been able to get in, in other words. (Not all Western ideas are good but we all know that some are.) Some factions forbid people to practice most Western ideas and to even be exposed to them, so there's been clashes, and even violence because of Western ideas.

Free countries are becoming more and more esteemed by certain other countries but this has much to do with economics and not culture. Some countries do not respect some of the morals they observe in free countries. This holds them back. They don't want people in their own country to learn Western ways and to be promiscuous, unfaithful to a spouse, disrespectful to parents, homosexual or lesbian, using drugs, and taking on the many various ways found in free countries (democracies). This is why they have some very strict laws in Muslim countries. Certain people living in the Free World hold to these stricter beliefs, too. The Muslims in these other countries have to realize this, but they do not embrace Western religions and ways. (Religion and ways can be two totally separate issues.)

Laws in the Free World protect people who participate in much of what has been noted about Western ways, but in some societies around the world, laws do not protect people who participate in much of what has been noted and observed in the Western world. No protective laws are in place and if you violate certain laws in any of those noted areas, you are in big trouble if you are in a Muslim country. Hindus and Buddhists can be pretty strict, too, especially Hindus. Some religions practice shunning. In some world religions there is still chauvinism and sexism. It is in most world religions, to be real.

Both (partners) in a marriage should want to put in an equal amount of effort, and to work equally as hard in a marriage. When something needs doing, whoever is free to do it should matter-of-factly do it so nothing gets overlooked and so there won't be any fighting. Both individuals in a marriage are of equal importance and should be given equal respect. Work should be divided up. To emphasize, respect is the glue of any relationship. Cutting a person down, belittling the other person or reducing them (making them feel small and unimportant), and not sharing in work or doing your part, some would say is actually evil. Any idleness and going off on unnecessary tangents will weaken and even ruin a relationship. Everything has to get done and can't stack up.

Human sexuality needs to be explored by all and it should begin at a relatively young age. Children and teenagers can go see counselors. A counselor can help anyone with this exploration, regardless of where someone is in life. Consider finding an actual sex therapist if you feel you need one. They tend to bring more activity into sessions, but everything is supposed to all be above board. There are many other issues in a marriage that a counselor can help people with, besides sex. Pretty much, the sky's the limit. Sometimes people will just go and see a counselor and just start talking. They may not even go for any particular reason. This can work just fine because usually what has been upsetting the person will come out. It is even possible to set up a structured program with a counselor so that certain subjects will come up, no matter what. This approach works for both solo clients and married couples.

Society has been changing. New laws have come in. New ways have entered society, and culture. But, some aspects of societies and cultures will always stay constant, at least for the mainstream. What some people try—be they young or old—may soon get out of that person's system and they'll go back to what they had previously thought or done before or they will go to something completely different. Transition goes on more, these days, because there are so many views and lifestyles.

People think for themselves more today. Young people are much more savvy and articulate. As new revelations come in, people modify or change what had been previous, or they build on to it. This can relate to sex in society, and also to marriages and other strong relationships. Life, itself, is kinetic and dynamic. Every day, there's something new to observe, hear, read about, try, and experience. Still, everything has a way of eventually settling in and then there are patterns and more stability, with the right guidance. There are life stages and a shifting into new life stages, which can be gradual. When a new life stage enters, it is best to be at a certain place in life. You want to be going up a progress ladder with regards to marriage, family, work, and the accumulation of ideas and adoption of values.

Do you think that everything you do during life stages is preparing people for what comes, after death? Many people do think that. Some people believe that there will be no marriage in Heaven, and absolutely no sex and that sex is only needed down here for conception and reproduction. Assuming that this is true, or even just possible, learning how to have a good sex life while on Earth should still be seen as being important and this is where a counselor can come in. Reading specially-selected books on the different aspects of marriage and partner relationships is always good but as noted before, such readings have to be sought out and appropriated. Set goals for your part in a relationship because goals help to give direction. Specificity is good. As a couple, talk things over and set goals together. Start with one goal or start with several. Periodically add a goal or two. They have to be realistic and be for the good of the relationship. A counselor can help clients with setting goals and with direction. Strong and loving relationships contribute positively to society, and to the world. The more there are the better the world will be.

There are several chapters relating to marriage and relationships in my relatively long book, *Counseling Helps*. The book has twenty-seven different helps in it so twenty-seven different topics are covered. At least a half to two-thirds of the helps relate more directly to marriage and problems in marriage or to other committed relationships. Some of the other ones relate to relationships and problems in relationships more indirectly, or they relate to couples that have specific problems. The rest of the helps cover topics that help the individual in more general ways. The helps help, in other words. That is why they are referred to as helps. In the title, the word, helps, has a double meaning.

The more a marriage or relationship is helped, the more chance there will be that sex will get better and stay good. Even politics is covered in that book, but not in the context of marriage. What is Democrat and what is Republican is compared and contrasted, rather thoroughly. I previously noted that both people in a committed relationship should share general political beliefs. They don't always have to be specific but the two should generally be aligned when it comes to political beliefs and also religious beliefs. It would be more ideal, if they were. Otherwise, the differences will put some extra stress on the marriage, especially at certain times (and those particular times can end out significantly hurting a marriage).

Today, many people are putting off marriage. They are either living alone or they are living with a partner that is same-sex or opposite-sex. Some people have roommates that are same-sex or opposite-sex and there is no romance going on with the roommates. There are a number of issues and circumstances around now that are dividing people. Also, the economic scenario is not strong for young people, who should really be thinking of finding a permanent life partner. It is all in the resolve. Young people have to work towards getting married and finding a life partner as a formal, thought-through goal. They have to live modestly, avoid debt if possible, get it all together, and get out and find a nice young man or nice young woman. They may have to keep their eyes wide open and look all around to find that person. They have to be on the look-out. They may have to step forward, at times, and make some kind of a play so they can get some time with someone they are interested in. It is not smart to play games, though. Do not start things off that way. Game playing often equals dishonesty, and also manipulation and deceptions.

When someone special is found, it will be foolish to play games. Always well treat that special person. Try to draw them in. Don't drive them away. Always be in a state of working, too—at home and, of course, at work. Push yourself to do what is extra, even when you are a little weary. This is what it's going to take to acquire even the basics, in this day and age. Get established. Set priorities. Why be concerned about having sex when there are other priorities? Young people will need to acquire an education or vocational training. Once a person is working, they are responsible and can take on more responsibilities.

Some say sex should only take place between working people—not older students and certainly not teen-aged students. This is a new thought. Should sex only be for working people because it should just be a privilege for people who are formally working? By the time people are working, they are very possibly considering marriage. This is a new thought that could and will be debated.

Relationships were forced into new situations when the coronavirus took over the world in 2020 because everybody had to stay home for an indefinite period of time. It was not a good time to go out looking for a partner or even new friends. For one thing, no one could get up close and personal with people. Even people who had an established partner were prone to stay clear of their partner if their partner went out and had to be around other people. Anyone could get the virus at any time, in other words. Sex and intimacy ceased or became much less in the various areas of world, especially where there were more virus cases. No one wanted to pass the virus to someone else or to have it get passed over to them so there were mass quarantines all over the world. You could, in some cases, be fined, when you ventured out. Many people died awful deaths from getting the coronavirus.

People were forced to be under the same roof for weeks and weeks, with no breaks away anyone else who lived under the same roof. Some people in the same household had to make efforts to avoid others in the home, which was not always so easy to do. It was quite unwise to get up close and personal with anybody. Some sexual relations had to stop, to be frank because no one ever knew if their partner had been exposed to the virus, since people could go around and be asymptomatic. Anyone could pick up the virus anywhere, too—at the grocery store, gas station, etc., and certainly at work if they were able to go to work because many were laid off or furloughed so they had to work at home and stay at home.

The expression, 'familiarity breeds contempt' can sometimes apply to people who are always around another person. When there is constant contact, or too much contact with another person, both people can get on each other's nerves. The excess contact can cause both to feel like they have less freedom and that they have crowded personal space, both physically and mentally. Two people, when put in a close and continual situation, can either get closer, or they can become less close than they had been. Going out to work every day causes two people to be separated but during the coronavirus epidemic, unemployment statistics went way up and no one really knew when they would return to work, or even if they would return to work. During the coronavirus pandemic, there was an increase in spousal abuse, and child abuse. The economic situation didn't help, nor did the constant close quarters. People who had children, especially really young children, had extra problems. Children and teenagers were not allowed to go to school. Parents had to teach, instruct, and spend time with their kids.

After the coronavirus hit, quite a few people were out of work. It put them out of work. Society and culture changed because of the coronavirus. There have been ideological shifts but old values centering on marriage and family stayed in place. In the end, everyone has to ask him or herself "what will make me most happy" and "how can I make other people happy—especially a life partner". With a life partner, that person will be around day in and day out so making the other person happy will be a continual endeavor. Sex can be a unifier and can add to the happiness of that other person.

Sex will always be important . . . all around the world. Sometimes, it is given too much emphasis. Sometimes, it is looked at all wrong. Neither situation is good. Sex is important, though. It will always be important but it has to be put in the right perspective and kept there. There are too many of the wrong kinds of ideas floating around about it, and not enough of the right kinds of ideas. This has become all too obvious and there are some people who could certainly be walking on a straighter path, when it concerns sex.

Sexual outlook has to be explored. Attitudes about sex have to, as well. There are diverse outlooks and attitudes in society, about sex. People should examine what their own are, from time to time. Sex trends in society can shift, and ebb and flow. Certain aspects about sex will never change, however. For a number of different reasons, it is good to be aware of what has been going on in the world of sex. We are all a part of society. We are all sexual beings. Sex lives can always be improved within the context of a relationship. Sex will always be a part of life.

# Reading and Sources

*Against Our Will: Men, Women and Rape*, Brownmiller, S., Simon and Schuster, New York, New York, 1975.

*Battered Wives*, Martin, D., Volcano Press, Inc., San Francisco, California, 1988.

*Building a Successful Marriage*, Landis, J., and M., Prentice-Hall, Inc., Englewood Cliffs, New Jersey, 1963.

*Conjugal Crime, Understanding and Changing the Wife-beating Pattern*, Davidson, T., Hawthorn Books, Inc., New York, NY, 1978.

*Coping with Your Grown Children*, Klingelhofer, Edwin L., PhD, Humand Press, Clifton, New Jersey, 1989.

*Counseling and Therapy for Couples*, Mark E., and Long, Lynn, L., Brooks/Cole Publications, Pacific Grove, California, 1998.

*Equal Marriage*, Bright, J., and R., Parthenon Press, Nashville, Tennessee, 1976.

*Human Intimacy: Marriage, the Family and Its Meaning*, Cox, Frank D., West Publishing Co., St. Paul, Minnesota, New York, New York, 1981.

*Human Sexuality: Opposing Viewpoints*, Stalcup, Brenda, Bruno, Leone, and Swisher, Karin, Greenhaven Press, San Diego, California, 1995.

*Intimacy and Alienation: Forms of Estrangement in Male/Female Relationships*, Garland Publishing, New York, New York, 2000.

*Kinsey*, American Experience Home Video—PBS, WGBN Educational Foundation, Paramount-Hollywood, California, 2005.

Kathy S. Thompson, M.A.

*Love and Sex in Marriage*, Deaton, J., Parker Publishing Co., Inc. West Nyack, New York, New York, 1978.

*Loving Styles: A Guide for Increasing Intimacy*, Rosenman, Martin F., Prentice-Hall, Inc., Englewood Cliffs, New Jersey 1979.

*Mental Illness in the Family: Issues and Trends,* Abosh, Beverley, and Collins, April, University of Toronto Press, Toronto, Ontario, Canada, 1996.

*Sex Addictions: Case Studies and Management,* Earle, Ralph, and Marcus R., and Osborn, Kevin, Brunner Mazel Pub. Co., New York, New York, 1995.

*Sex Therapy: A Practical Guide*, Hawton, Keith, Oxford University Press, Oxford, England, New York, New York, 1985.

*Sexual Preference: Its Development in Men and Women.* Bell, A., Weinberg, M., Hamemrsmith, S., Indiana University Press, Bloomington, Indiana, 1981.

*Sexuality,* Nye, Robert, Oxford University Press, Oxford, England, New York, New York, 1999.

*Strange Loves: The Human Aspects of Sexual Deviation*, Chesser, E., William Morrow and Co., Inc., New York, NY, 1971.

*Supercouple Syndrome*, Sotile, Wayne M. and Mary O. John Wiley & Sons, Inc., New York, New York, 1998.

*The Goals of Human Sexuality*, Singer, I., W. W. Norton and Co., Inc., New York, New YOrk, 1973.

*The Facts of Love, Comfort, A., and J.,* Ballantine Books, New York, New York, 1979.

*The Kahn Report on Sexual Preferences*, Kahn, Sandra S., St. Martin's Press, New York, New York, 1981.

*The Intimate Enemy*, Bach, G., Wyden, P., William Morrow and Co., New York, New York, 1969.

*The Psychology of Sex Differences*, Lips, H., Colwill, N., Prentice-Hall Inc., Englewood Cliffs, New Jersey, 1978.

*Therapeutic Counseling,* Bramer, L., Shostrom, E., Prentice-Hall Co., Englewood Cliffs, New Jersey, 1968.

*Today's Neurotic Family,* Tashman M.D., H. New York University Press, New York, New York, 1957.

*What Comes After You Say I Love You?*, Hine, James R., Pacific Books, Palo Alto, California, 1980.

# *Index*

perpetrators  12
perps  12, 16
persecution  88
personal value system  96
perspective  24, 36, 74, 93–96, 100, 108, 115
perversion  15
Phil Donahue  62
philosophy  87
physical abuse  69
physical attraction  98
physical relationship  7
physical weakness  48
physical work  46
physiological  36, 45–46
physiology  103
pill  49
Pillow Talk  65
pimp  30
planning  84, 99
plastic surgery  29
platonic  98
pleasure  52–53
police  17–18, 32, 67
political  27–28, 42–43, 87, 113
political belief  87, 113
political choices  42
political leanings  43
politics  28, 87, 113
pollution  110
polygamy  110
population  7, 26, 92, 107, 110
population growth  110
population increase  26, 110
porn images  13
pornographic  14, 45, 104
pornography  13–15, 17, 44, 50
positives  39, 41, 69, 82, 95
potters  61
Povitch  62
Povitch, Maury  62
practical  42, 47, 55
prayer  92
pregnancies  36, 106
pregnancy  36–37, 53

pregnant  85, 91
pre-marital counseling  97, 101
pre-marital sex  106
pressure  7, 10, 13, 35, 70, 91
pretense  7, 63
Pretty Woman  19
pride  31, 73, 75
prideful  70, 73, 77
principles  9, 30, 92
prison  14, 33
private  17, 20, 107–108
private diseases  20
problem  12, 26, 41, 44–46, 59, 67, 71, 90, 99, 103, 108
problems  7, 12, 19, 29, 35, 38, 40, 45–46, 49, 51, 56, 59–61, 65–67, 69, 71, 73, 78, 87, 92, 95, 98–99, 101–102, 108, 113, 115
procreate  90
procreation  53
program  11, 36, 51, 85–86, 102, 112
progress  94, 97, 112
promiscuity  7, 36, 103
promiscuous  111
promotions  47
property  110
prosecute  14
prostitute  18–19
prostitutes  18–19
prostitution  18
protection  69
protective  23–24, 111
protectors  69
Protestant  88
Psychiatrist  103
psychological  3, 14, 16, 29, 36, 45–46, 51, 86, 105
Psychologist  103
Psychology  118
psychopath  14
psychopaths  14
public  3, 5, 17, 24, 31–33, 106, 110
public bathrooms  32
public sympathy  24
Public sympathy  24

Printed in the United States
by Baker & Taylor Publisher Services